Theology Reformed and Reforming

Theology Reformed and Reforming

edited by

Peter McEnhill

2008
Theology in Scotland
St Andrews

Theology in Scotland
St Mary's College
University of St Andrews
St Andrews KY16 9JU
Scotland

ISBN 978-0-9559115-0-7

Designed and typeset by the University of St Andrews Reprographics Unit

The University of St Andrews is a charity registered in Scotland, No: SC013532

CONTENTS

Acknowledgments

These essays derive from a conference organised by the Cheshunt Institute for Reformed Studies at Westminster College, Cambridge, on the 'Future of Reformed Theology'. I am grateful to the participants and contributors to that conference for their patience in waiting for its results to appear in some tangible form. I am grateful too for the gracious way in which the various contributors gave of their time, talents and not inconsiderable personal charm to that project. It was a wonderful occasion. Sadly, Professor Colin Gunton of course has died in the period between the conference and the publication of this volume of essays. He was a much valued participant at the proceedings and a wise and valued adviser to the Cheshunt Institute for Reformed Studies. His contribution to the world of theological scholarship is sorely missed.

As the then Director of the Cheshunt Institute for Reformed Studies I was immensely privileged to play a very small part in the never ending process that is the rethinking of the Reformed faith in our particular place at our particular time. We do not believe for a moment that we have issued the last word, or even a particularly definitive word on Reformed theology in this set of essays. They are merely contributions to the 'conversations on the way' as we seek to discern what God is saying to his Church today. They are, I think, useful promptings for discussion.

Formal acknowledgement and thanks must be recorded in the way of things at this point, though in truth, they rarely adequately suffice in testifying to the many kindnesses received. Colleagues at Westminster College have been resolute in their support of the whole enterprise and so I thank, David Cornick, then Principal, whose idea the whole institute was; John Proctor as ever on hand with sage advice; Lance Stone, good friend and a wise and knowing contributor throughout the whole affair and someone who listened to a lot of my pre-conference gripes over the occasional pint; Janet Tollington, as always a rock in terms of organisation and efficiency. So too the administrative staff, working behind the scenes, but always so important to the whole enterprise must also be thanked and I record my gratitude to Marilyn Russell, Lyn Woodfield and Margaret Thomson.

Elsewhere in Cambridge and beyond, Jeremy Morris shared the burden of organising a similar type of conference and arranging publication over a similar period – so we shared birth pains together often over a soothing libation – though he got his book out quicker than me. So too with Ben Quash whose good humour and sagacity in matters theological seems to admit of no limitations. Former students, now colleagues and friends, Peter Stevenson and Jason Askew were great figures of support, assistance and enthusiasm during the actual conference itself. In Scotland George Newlands and Bill Shaw were always on hand for encouragement and advice. Bill in particular with the support of Theology in Scotland was indispensable in bringing this volume into existence. Colin Bovaird, production manager of Theology in Scotland must also be thanked for his contribution to the end product.

More formal expressions of gratitude must go to the Hope Trust for their financial support in relation to the production of this volume. And also to the 'Drummond Trust, 3 Pitt Terrace, Stirling' for their welcome support too. The willingness of both organisations to support the production of works in Reformed theology is greatly appreciated in these straitened times. And so too for the various permissions that have been granted for the production of related articles produced elsewhere subsequent to our conference. To Continuum Press for the permissions that have been granted for reproducing the conference presentations of Colin Gunton and Duncan Forrester which later appeared in *Intellect and Action: Elucidations on Christian Theology and the Life of Faith*, C. E. Gunton, Edinburgh: T. & T. Clark, 2000, ISBN 0567 087352, chapter nine, pp. 156–73; and *Truthful Action: Explorations in Practical Theology*, D. B. Forrester, Edinburgh: T. & T. Clark, 2000, ISBN 0 567 087476, chapter 11, pp. 161–84. Grateful thanks must also be expressed to Ashgate Press for allowing us to reprint Alan Sell's conference paper later published in *Testimony and Tradition: Studies in Reformed and Dissenting Thought*, Aldershot, Hants.; Burlington, Vt.: Ashgate, 2004: "Reformed Theology: Whence and Whither", Chapter 10, pp. 233–252. To the Calvin Studies Society who also reproduced Brian Gerrish's paper in *The Legacy of John Calvin*, ed. David Foxglover, Grand Rapids, Mich.: CRC Product Services, 2000. Also to Chalis Press for the right to use the conference presentation of Walter Brueggemann later printed as chapter two of *The Faithfulness of Otherwise*, Chalis Press, 2001, pp. 27–43, ISBN 9780827236400. Similarly, Eberhard's Busch paper has been subsequently revised in his *Die Gemeinde von Brudern und Schwestern*, in: ders., Reformiert. Profil einer Konfession. Zurich 2007, Kap. 8. C 2007 Theologischer Verlag Zurich.

And finally to my family, my wife Linda, my daughter Jennifer Anne and my son Peter Ewen, together they humour me, puncture my pomposity, struggle with my interest in the strange and weird prognostications of theology, but always they are a delight and a source of joy, as such they ground me in the truly important and enduring things of life. To them I owe a debt beyond calculation or measure.

PETER MCENHILL

INTRODUCTION

The Future of the Reformed Tradition

Gathering a collection of scholars to discuss the ongoing and future significance of the Reformed tradition is a somewhat perilous undertaking in these troubled days. For there is no *one* understanding of the Reformed enterprise, nor even much common agreement as to the way ahead (see Alan Sell's article in this volume for an elaboration of this point). Nor is there a single confessional statement that would command the agreement of the majority of churches that make up the Reformed family today – although we might all be able to produce similar lists of what would constitute certain *historically* definitive summations of the essentials of the Reformed faith. Alan Sell has even gone so far as saying that there are not as many as five doctrines that are 'Reformed' in the sense that they distinctively belong to the Reformed tradition and not to other branches of the Christian Church.

No doubt *sola fide, solus Christus, sola scriptura, sola gratia* and *soli Deo gloria* remain bedrock affirmations (though very variously interpreted, and if we think of Schleiermacher and Jonathan Edwards as being opposite and limiting poles of Reformed theology, you will see what I mean) of any genuinely Reformed theology and they are all touched upon at different points in this collection of articles. But in an ecumenical age would we say that they belong to 'the Reformed' in any exclusive sense, or do they appropriately and correctly represent 'catholic' truth as one might expect if they are truly derived from scripture? Would we even say that in this post-modern, post-Christendom, globalised and plural world that we interpret them in precisely the same way as our illustrious forefathers (and mothers) did? Our context is inescapably different from theirs, and if there is one truism about Reformed theology it is that it has long revealed the profoundly contextual nature of its own brand of theology, and implicitly therefore of *all* theology.

Can a tradition and theology formed almost parochially to meet the needs of the city-state churches of Zurich and Geneva (to take up only its most classical expressions) continue to have relevance in the modern situation?

1

What endures and what must pass away in the new context that we are facing? It is almost five hundred years since the birth of the Reformation and everywhere we look in the northern hemisphere the mainline churches of the Reformed tradition are in numerical decline. Some are even predicting the demise of the classical 'Reformed' enterprise in this generation. Only in the 'global South' do we find Reformed churches that are thriving and growing to a significant degree (provided Korea is regarded as belonging to the 'global South'). But how much longer such churches will explicitly identify themselves as 'Reformed' in a post-confessional and post-denominational age is open to question – and maybe that is no bad thing.

Therefore, it is almost a commonplace to observe these days that one can discern a crisis of identity among the Reformed whenever one attends a gathering of that tradition. What is it to be Reformed today? What is its continuing relevance? If, as we observed earlier, there are not as many as five doctrines that are distinctly and uniquely Reformed in the sense that they belong to us and no-one else, what then constitutes our distinctive identity? Surely, not polity, for there is no single agreed polity that is common to all Reformed churches, though there is a definitive preference for conciliar forms of government and the dispersal of power. Moreover, in an ecumenical age, a distinctive church order seems an inadequate basis on which to found our identity. Few, if any, uniting churches which have brought together Reformed and Episcopal systems of church order have ended up exhibiting much by way of Reformed polity after the union. And therein lies the rub, because a professed weakness of institutional identity will always tend to mean that it is the Reformed party that will 'give way' on issues of order when confronted by a tradition which has a much firmer attachment to the divine ordination of its structures.

Is that important? Only in as much as the ongoing legitimacy of our separate existence as a family of churches surely depends on us representing some essential point of the gospel that would otherwise be lost if we were not testifying to it by our distinctive presence. Calvin famously argued that 'where the Word is truly preached and heard and the sacraments observed according to the Word of God, there a church of God exists.' And he also warned against needless separation from such a true church which exhibited those marks. As we no longer exist in the polemical spirit of former times that would have denied the proper legitimacy of certain other churches, if we in effect acknowledge that within them the word is 'truly preached and heard' and the sacraments are 'properly administered', what then legitmises our continued separate existence? Perhaps the Reformed witness in this ecumenical age will be found in its willingness to lay down and lose its life, to abandon any false security based on its historic forms and identity, in order to find true life in a more expansive and richer understanding of the Church?

But perhaps this crisis in Reformed identity is not therefore a symptom of failure, but paradoxically of the success of the Reformed enterprise? Is it the case that the ideas which the Reformers came out and fought for long ago have now become widely dispersed and accepted in one form or another throughout the universal Church? Certainly there is one reading of Vatican II, to take but one example, that would see that Council as the point when many of the impulses of the Protestant tradition were recognised and accepted by the Roman Catholic Church (albeit absorbed quite properly within their own framework of thought). Perhaps then the Reformed tradition is experiencing some form of crisis because the work it arose to do is complete and that the issues which the Reformers separated for are now broadly accepted throughout Christ's Church? That is perhaps to go too far, but it is interesting to speculate what would now constitute 'church dividing' issues between us if the Church was in fact still one undivided entity today.

But, if there is no one doctrine that is uniquely Reformed, perhaps our identity lies in the precise way that a particular constellation of doctrines are held and exhibited as forms of life – a matter of tenor and tone if you like. Certainly it would be difficult for the Reformed sensibility to abandon its commitment to the absolute freedom and sovereignty of God in his gracious works towards the world – the famed 'priority of grace'. And it remains true that any suggestion that God is somehow bound up entirely within the ministry, operation and mission of the Church and its particular orders is somewhat alien to the Reformed spirit. For, as the Second Helvetic Confession has it, God is not bound to the Church or its signs, 'For we know that God had some friends in the world that were not of the commonwealth of Israel.' And a radical commitment to that freedom of God in a globalised multi-cultural age is perhaps a distinctive Reformed emphasis that still needs to be asserted today. For God's mission to the world is broader than the mission of the Church and the operation of his grace cannot be narrowly confined to its structures or ministries.

Thus the sovereignty of God and the integrity of his creation are traditional

Reformed themes that thrust themselves forward as being of particular relevance in the contemporary context. To be sure they are not uniquely Reformed doctrines, but again a radical commitment to them and to the implication drawn from them that society should be transformed according to the demands of Christ and his Kingdom has been a particularly important theme within the Reformed tradition. In a world of desperate inequality, poverty, hunger and conflict, threatened by an irresistible and restless urge to consume even creation itself, surely these themes need to be rediscovered and made relevant in a powerful fashion for today? The issues of justice and peace, the formation of communities of nurture and inclusion and the integrity of the natural order are all rooted directly in the proclamation of the sovereignty of God.

The Reformed tradition is not yet then a spent force and there is much vitality left in it and in the resources of its theological tradition. That is why we decided to hold a conference on Reformed theology and its ever renewable task. The articles presented here are not then the final word on the subject for the conversation is ongoing and will not cease for some time yet. However, they are useful prompters for discussion on the way.

PETER McENHILL

1

THE FUTURE OF REFORMED THEOLOGY

Jürgen Moltmann

I am really not sure whether I am the right person to speak about the future of Reformed theology, because old as I am I shall certainly not see that future when it comes. Would it not have been better to ask a young, promising theologian, to tell what future he or she would wish or hope for Reformed theology?

I am not a future-teller who can look into the unknown future and tell what we have to expect. The only thing we know for sure about the future is that it mostly comes differently from what we have thought. The future is full of surprises and disappointments. And we also know that coming generations will do things differently than what we had wished. After all, we did the same with our fathers and predecessors – to their dismay and their surprise.

There is however another question: What is Reformed theology of the twentieth century leaving to theology in the twenty-first century? What unsolved problems are we presenting to the coming generations, and what unfulfilled promises? What investments have we made in their future, and what debts are we leaving behind for them to pay? What will the coming generations praise us for, and for what will they criticise us?

If we are entering a post-confessional age, has then Reformed theology had its time and has it already made itself superfluous? If we live more and more in the 'broad-house' of an ecumenical church, because the people don't care anymore about denominational specialities and differences, do we really still need Lutheran, Methodist, Baptist, Roman Catholic and Reformed theologies? Are the new alliances and the new differences in theology still following the old confessional lines? I don't think so. For we have fundamentalist and liberal or modernist trends in all denominations and theological camps. So what has Reformed theology still to contribute to the 'common house' of ecumenical, or simply Christian, theology so that we must care for the 'Reformed' character of theology and respect it? What is our contribution to a universal theology for the common future of the Christian churches, the world religions, the groaning creation and the coming of God?

I Theologia Reformata et Semper Reformanda

Let me start with the simple question: How does Reformed theology understand its own name and in what sense do we claim to be 'Reformed'? Reformed theologians have asked again and again: What was the Reformation, what is it to *be* Reformed and what *must* be Reformed, and by what criterion Church and theology were, are, and should be, Reformed? These questions are typical for reforming processes. Unlike Lutheran theology with its *Book of Concord*, Reformed theology is not grounded in a confessional statement laid down once and for all. Unlike Roman Catholic theology it is not based on a tradition of 'infallible and irreformable' (as *Vaticanum I* said) papal doctrinal decisions and morally definitive statements. It is simple but true: Reformed theology is grounded in the '*Reformation of the Church according to the Word of God*', attested in Holy Scripture, preached every new day and confessed anew in each new situation. With respect to the Word of God, the Reformed church was not born in the Reformation period, but is as old as the Apostles and the Apostolic witnesses and is in continuity with the ancient church and in solidarity with the churches worldwide. The Word of God, attested in the Scripture, makes the Reformed church and theology universally relevant. What does this say?

Reformed theology is, as the name testifies, nothing but *reformatory theology*, the theology of the *permanent reformation* of the Church, of Christian life in the world – and the world itself. To be sure, reformatory theology owes its existence and its dynamics to the unique Reformation of the sixteenth century, but this is more than a historical memory and other than just a historical tradition. Reformed theologians have always lived in grateful community with Calvin, Zwingli, Bucer and Melanchthon, and of course with Martin Luther. But there has never been any personality cult as in Lutheranism with its article of faith *De vocatione Dr. Martini Lutheri*. Reformed theologians have always refused to call a church after the name of its human 'founder', because it is founded in Christ. Apart from the 'Kimbanguist Church' in the Congo, the 'Lutheran Church' is the only

Christian church called with a human name.[1]

Reformatory theology is theology in the service of reformation. Reformation is its leading and orientating principle. It makes reformed theology into a *permanent reforming theology*. Just as the life of a Christian is, according to the first of Luther's ninety-five theses of 1517, a 'perpetual penance', so reformatory theology is a constant turning around from the past to the future, more precisely, to the future of God's kingdom promised by the Word of God. It is not historically known who invented this formula, but it accurately describes the principle of Church and theology reformed by God's Word: *ecclesia reformata et semper reformanda*. This is true also for theology: *theologia reformata et semper reformanda*. Tradition and innovation are one single process and can't be separated. Therefore 'Reformation' is not a one-time event in the past, to which confessionalists can appeal and traditionalists could rest upon. Innovation starts not from utopia and point zero, but grasps us where we are and motivates us in what we are. Reformation 'according to God's Word' is *permanent reformation*, that is to say, a dynamic that keeps Church and theology breathless with suspense, infusing Church and theology with the passion for the kingdom. Reformation is in our understanding a story that is constantly making history an event that can't be concluded in this world, a process that will reach its fulfilment in the *parousia* of Christ. This means for a theology which is rooted in God's Word of promise that it will be *theologia semper reformanda usque ad finem*. The historically-promised future of the 'coming God' is forming Reformed theology into an eschatologically-oriented theology.

There is also another respect in which Reformed theology is *reformatory theology*: it is not only concerned with the reformed church, but beyond this with the *reformation of the whole of life*. Very soon after the first decades of the historical reformations in Europe, the call for a 'second Reformation' was heard. After the Reformation of the preaching and teaching of the Church, a 'Reformation of Life', which would complete the first Reformation, was demanded. Not only the Church, but also the vocations of Christians in public life and by this, also politics and economics were to be brought under the mandates of the gospel. This 'Second Reformation', the 'Reformation of Life', spread among German countries and cities through the Palatinate Church Order and the Heidelberg Catechism of 1563, written by the Calvinist theologian, Olevian, and the Melanchthonian, Ursin.

The congregation's *façon de vivre* was characterized by what is called

'Church discipline', frequently acquiring a typically Calvinistic legalism. This *'Gesetzlichkeit'* has been thoroughly criticised already, so that perhaps we should also see the positive side: Church discipline often kept the congregations in faith during time of persecution, 'under the cross' as Johannes a Lasco described the refugee congregations of the lower Rhine. Why? Because confessing Christ and following Christ belong together; if the act of faith is really an all-encompassing act of living, and not a half-hearted one. *Solus Christus* is the content of the confessing faith, *totus Christus* is the life of the faithful. No one can truly recognize Christ unless s/he follows him in his/her life (Hans Denk, the Anabaptist).

Finally, Reformed theology is reformatory theology in a universal respect: it concerns the *reformatio mundi*, the reformation of the world according to the will of God. I think it was first Amos Comenius in the seventeenth century, who coined this formula, but it aptly describes the intentions of Reformed theology from the beginning with respect to the state, society, culture and nature. Not only the Church's witness and life, as well as the life of Christians in the world, but all areas of life are to be reformed according to the creative, liberating and redeeming Word, for God is God, unbounded and all-encompassing: 'The earth is the Lord's and all that is in it, the world and they that dwell therein' (Psalm 24:1). Reformed theology has always understood the divinity of God as God's sovereignty and consequently theocratic and universal, whether as the all-determining reality or the reality which supports all things, whether as the transcendental sovereignty of God or as the spiritual presence of God the Spirit, whose energies are poured out over all flesh. Therefore what is to be reformed according to God's Word and Spirit cannot be limited to certain areas of life, be they religious or moral spaces. *Reformatio mundi* here and now is the *anticipation* of the *new creation* which Christ will consummate on his day (Uppsala 1968).

II *Reformed Theology on the Threshold of Modern History*

The second generation

The formation of Reformed theology began with the second generation of reformers in the sixteenth century. The first generation was prophetic and made the breakthrough; the second generation formed the new church. Both belong together: Luther and Melanchthon; Farel and Calvin; Zwingli and Bucer. What would be the first without the second? The first had the prophetic vision and the polemics, the second the task of ordering the new in church, in school and in public life. Martin Luther proclaimed the rediscovered gospel and was most effective through his translation of the Bible into German and his catechisms, but only Philipp Melanchthon wrote the first Protestant theology in his *Loci Communes* of 1521, which he enlarged again and again. Zwingli was strong in his disputations in Zürich and convinced the city council, but only Heinrich Bullinger's *Hausbuch* and his treatise on *De Testamento seu Foedere Dei Unico et Aeterno* of 1534 formed the typically Züricher tradition of federal theology. Farel was an enthusiastic preacher, but only John Calvin founded the Geneva tradition of Reformed theology through his grand work *Institutio Christianae Religionis*, published in ever enlarged forms. With these names of the second generation we have already the three main sources of Reformed theology at hand: the Calvin tradition from Geneva with far-reaching influence in Western Europe; the Bullinger tradition with influence in Northern Europe and England; and the 'German-Reformed' tradition, which some Lutherans called 'Cryptocalvinism', but was in fact Melanchthonian, in the German countries.

Seen from a sociological perspective: Reformed theology grew up in the city-reformations 'from below', so to speak, not in the feudal-reformations (*Fürstenreformationen*) 'from above' under the law: '*Cujus regio – ejus religio*'. Reformed Christianity was to a large extent a 'voluntary religion', not an established or prescribed religion. The Reformed catechisms are not people's catechisms, but more short theological books for higher education in Gymnasiums and the Gymnasium *illustre*. The Reformed belief was historically attractive for the educated people in the advanced West European countries – France, the Netherlands, England, and later the USA. Reformed universities such as Herborn and Leyden attracted students from all over Eastern Europe. I am saying this not in order to boast in the advanced status of Reformed theology, but to explain why Reformed theology was again and again present and effective at the epochal thresholds of modern history and formed in its own way the decisive steps of modern and post-modern life.

At the birth of the modern world

The age between the post-Reformation period and the beginning of the modern world is still mostly unknown. But it is exactly in this age that Reformed theology formed the transitions and influenced the spirit and life-style of the people. I shall pick up only two ideas which were and have been influential until the present day: (a) the discovery of the *subjectivity* of human beings; (b) the idea of the *covenant*, which led to the developing politics of democracy.

(a) *The discovery of the subject*: The modern world began when people no longer followed the collective patterns of their status, but discovered the dignity and rights of the individual and took their life in their own hands. This started within religious movements in England. The seventeenth century saw the rise of the 'religions of subjectivity': Quakers with the 'inner light of the soul'; Baptists with the personal decision of faith; Methodists with their 'heart-warming experience' of Christ. 'Soul-liberty' was Roger Williams' keyword for claiming religious freedom for the individual in New England. One can also speak of the rise of Pietism all over the Protestant world. The roots however for Protestant Pietism and the new religions of subjectivity are to be found long before Fox and Wesley and Spener and Francke in the Reformed tradition, and here especially in the Netherlands. This was Gisbert Voet and the life-style of Precisement ('Präzisheit') and Wilhelm Amesius. Jean de Labadie influenced the mysticism in the Reformed tradition, which later Gerhard Tersteegen in the Rhineland propagated in hymns and poems, still powerful in German hymnbooks today. In England it was Richard Baxter and emergent Puritanism that was influential. The theological background can surely be found in the Reformed doctrine of predestination. That believers are the elected ones certainly strengthened their individual self-esteem and their freedom over against the institutions of church, state and class society. Joseph Bohatec (*England und die Geschichte der Menschen- und Bürgerrechte*, 1956) has shown the enormous public influence of these religious movements on the formation of the growing egalitarian bourgeois society and the coming democratic revolution with the vision: 'All people are created free and equal.'

Max Weber created his famous/infamous thesis out of the historical connections on the affinity of 'Calvinism and Capitalism' (*Dieprotestantische Ethik und der Geist des Kapitalismus*, 1904). He wanted to counter Karl

Marx and prove that the economy could not only influence the spirit as 'Überbau', but that the spirit could also influence the economy. In our case, the Calvinist doctrine of predestination and the puritanical notion of vocation engendered a 'disinhibiting effect on the capitalistic striving for profit.' The 'inner-worldly asceticism' of Calvinists recognized by one's own economic success as a mark of being 'chosen', using the method of the *syllogismus practicus*. Max Weber was right in seeing the affinity of the rising religious subjectivity and the growing capitalism, but he was wrong in making Calvinism responsible for capitalism. The great repositories of capital in the sixteenth century remained Catholic; the exploitation of the newly-discovered territories in America and the profitable slave trade from Africa rested in the hands of the Catholic kings of Spain and Portugal. It was the shift of trade from the Mediterranean and the Baltic sea to the Atlantic which favoured the Netherlands and England. And last, but not least, Weber's best proofs for his thesis are from Benjamin Franklin, who lived 200 years after Calvin in the USA. Weber likes to quote Franklin's famous dictum: 'Get what you can, save what you can ...', but he stops before it goes on to say 'and give what you can'. He had no interest in the social work of the Reformed churches and communities. One can therefore easily defend the counter-theses of 'Calvinism and Socialism.'

(b) *The idea of the covenant*: The second significant contribution of Reformed theology to the formation of the modern era lies in unity of covenantal theology and covenantal politics. Reformed federal theology is commonly attributed to Johannes Coccejus (1603–69), but goes back to Bullinger's seminal tractate of 1534. Bullinger saw God's one eternal covenant with humankind, established with Abraham, formed through Moses with Israel and fulfilled in Christ, foretold by the prophets, proclaimed by the apostles, as the centre of the Holy Scriptures and the heart of biblical theology. Coccejus distinguished a series of covenants, from Adam to Christ, which succeeded and superseded each other, preparing the way for the coming kingdom of God. This was a kind of *'heilsgeschichtliche' Theologie* on the basis of a 'prophetic', i.e. historical, exegesis of the scriptures. God's covenant includes religious as well as civil life, human as well as earthly life. Reformed federal theology originated in Zürich, was developed in the Netherlands and Scotland and brought to New England and Hungary. The covenant idea was probably more influential than the doctrine of predestination, because it was related to the presbyteral-synodal church order as well as to democratic municipal constitutions of free cities, the Swiss confederation, the Hanseatic League and the covenants of Scottish clans.

Reformed covenantal politics was first articulated in the *Vindiciae contra tyrannos* (1579), written probably by Philippe du Plessis-Mornay in reaction to the horrors of that barbaric St. Bartholomew's night in Paris in 1572, when the leading Huguenots, assembled in Paris, were murdered by the Catholic 'rex christianissimus.' Mornay's *Vindiciae* tried to answer the practical political questions: Do subjects owe obedience to a ruler, whose decrees contradict the law of God? Is one compelled to resist a ruler who breaks God's law? Are neighbouring rulers permitted to intervene on behalf of suffering subjects, not their own? Very modern questions in matters of human rights! His answer is based on the idea of the double covenant of the Bible: the first covenant is made between God and his people; the second between the people and their king, transferring their sovereignty to him. If the sovereign breaks the covenant with the people, the people are free of any obligation; if he breaks the covenant of God with the people, the people have to resist. 'Resistance to tyrants is obedience to God.' This political idea includes the concept that political sovereignty comes from the people, with whom God has made his covenant. The right of the people to resistance was the basis of covenantal and democratic constitutional states – and still is. Johannes Althusius published the *Politica methodice digesta* in Herborn at the beginning of the seventeenth century, taking the ideas of the *Vindiciae* further: politics is not just power and sovereignty, but the *ars consociandi*, bonding and binding together people with mutual agreements and commitments, for humans are social creatures: *symbiotes*, not 'wolves' that must be tamed with repression.

Compared with Jean Bodin's and Thomas Hobbes' political theories of the (absolutistic) Leviathan, we see that the Reformed theologians and political scientists used a *positive* anthropology in order to keep political power under the control of the people, while they used a *negative* anthropology in order to justify the unlimited power of the sovereign. If man is by nature an anarchist, a 'wolf', or a sinner, he needs the strong hands of authoritarian rulers. If man is justified by God's covenant and worthy of this covenant and able to promise commitments and receive trust, only a government 'of the people, by the people and for the people' is legitimate. The political federalists around James Madison in the USA learned from the theological federalist John Witherspoon. We can easily see in the dignity of a democratic constitution the religious dimension of the covenant.

On the way to a postmodern world

The Reformation took place in the *Corpus Christianum*. The 'modern world' was a composition of faith and culture, church and state, Christian and civil community, Christianity and European Christendom, *Cristianidad*. The nineteenth century was called 'The Christian Century', and the progressive world named 'the Christian World'. All the imperial powers – Great Britain, the USA, France, Prussian-Germany, Austria-Hungary and Russia – were Christian powers. One expected the Christianization of the rest of the world with the globalisation of these superpowers 'in this generation', as John Mott proclaimed. But then came the fundamental catastrophe of the twentieth century: World War One, where the nations that were above all the foremost examples of the 'Christian State', those exemplars of cultural Christianity, those then superpowers of the age destroyed themselves in an orgy of destruction lasting four years. The first who saw that this was the end of the modern Christian world were – in Germany – the dialectical theologians, first of all Karl Barth. They recognized the end of '*Kulturprotestantismus*' and worked for the resurrection of the Church of Christ out of the ruins of the 'Christian world'. Against the reduction of Christian theology to a science of religion or of Christian cultural history, Karl Barth erected his monumental *Kirchliche Dogmatik*. Christian theology is '*kirchliche Wissenschaft*', not a science of religion. The coin was still unknown, but Barth and his followers made the first step from the modern to a post-modern age.

Tillich spoke at that time about a 'theology of crisis'; Barth, Bultmann, Brunner and Gogarten of a theology of the 'Word of God'. A renaissance of reformatory theology came to pass in the twentieth century; Luther and Calvin were all of a sudden present again. Barth defended in the first period of 'dialectical theology' the idea of God as the 'Wholly Other', who shatters all human expectations and shapes all religious feelings, and forcefully asserted that God is in Godself the crisis of the human world. In the second edition of the *Commentary on Romans* published in 1921, it is the infinite qualitative difference between God and humankind, which produces the crisis of the human world. In the *Christian Dogmatics* of 1927 and the *Church Dogmatics* of 1932 ff, it is the absolute sovereignty of God in God's self-revelation as 'Lord' and not the religious needs of a pious self-consciousness, but solely the divinity of God and the honour due his name that provide certainty in an uncertain world and an anchor in history without moorings. Barth was not against culture, but he saw the Church, 'who hears God's word alone', as far removed from culture as from barbarism. From 1921 on, however, he discovered analogies, parables and metaphors in culture, in politics and in nature to the kingdom of God testified to by the Church. The world is able and in need of correspondences to the kingdom of God. There can and must be correspondences between divine and human justice. With his seminal essays on *"Kirche und Kultur," "Rechtfertigung und Recht,"* and *"Christengemeinde und Bürgergemeinde,"* Barth followed the lines of Zwingli and Calvin and avoided the separation of the 'two kingdoms' in the Lutheran tradition, a separation which misled Friedrich Gogarten in the Hitler-Reich. Barth, even with all his early criticism of the Christian world, never became a theologian of the *'diastasis,'* of a fundamentalist retreat into the 'strong fortress' of the Church against 'the world.' He inspired the resistance of the Confessing Church against Hitler, the Nazis and their slaves the 'German Christians' after 1933 and formulated the Barmen Theological Declaration in 1934. This standpoint is in accord with the best of the Reformed traditions: God's Word and the independent and resisting Church of Christ; the Kingdom of God and the new obedience in the whole life; creative righteousness in analogy; and correspondence to the righteousness of God. With his theology Barth began a new reformation, but the churches in Europe have not yet caught up with his vision.

III *Unsolved Problems*

The strong points of Reformed theology are at the same time her weaknesses. In order to become fit for the twenty-first century in the 'common-house' of ecumenical theology and in the universal life of humankind on earth, it seems to be necessary to reformulate the strength of the Reformed tradition. Here I am just summarizing a few questions and sharpening them for discussion's sake:

The elected ones and the massa perditionis

Since Calvin and Beza, 'Calvinism' is famous on the one hand and notoriously accused on the other hand for the doctrine of the double predestination (*predestinatio gemina*). This belief was and has been a great strength of

Reformed Christians and it gave them an invincible certainty in their faith to know that one is not only justified by the grace and sanctified by the glory, but also elected by the will of God. From this belief in the divine election follows the trust in the divine perseverance (*perseverantia sanctorum usque ad finem*): I shall not fall and nobody and nothing can tear me out of the hands of God. This belief was the power of resistance in persecution. Marie Durand's '*recister*' carved in the Tour de la Constance at Aigues-Mortes reminds us and requires our respect. But does this means that the rest of humankind is lost and damned in eternity as the *massa perditionis*, as the Augustinian-Calvinist tradition tells us? Must we tell the rest of the world, 'According to the Bible those who do not believe in Christ will perish,' as Choan-Seng Song asks, 'Is there no salvation outside the Church?'[2] Are the other religions just false religions, demonic and idolatrous? It is certainly not the gospel to confront other people with the statement 'You belong to the *massa perditionis*.' It is certainly not in the Spirit of God to condemn ninety-five per cent of the people God has created in his image, and it seems not in accordance with the Spirit of Christ to limit his salvation to a few elect people for whom he died. The doctrine of the double predestination – here the election, there the condemnation – is however not worse than the modern pelagian doctrine of the double end of human free choice – heaven for believers, hell, or the more modern 'non-being,' for unbelievers. Is hell the result of a divine decision or of a human decision, condemnation from above or 'the ultimate affirmation of the reality of human freedom' from below.[3]

I think neither/nor, and would follow at this point the ingenious chris-tological reformulation of the Reformed doctrine of double predestination offered by Karl Barth in *Church Dogmatics* II/2. Because God has put his righteous condemnation of sin, evil and death on Jesus Christ, and Christ has suffered the eternal death for all on his cross, where he cried, 'My God, why have you forsaken me?', with Christ's resurrection eternal death and hell, sin and condemnation are overcome and the unconditional and univer-sal election by grace (*Gnadenwahl*) is to be proclaimed to all and everyone. 'The doctrine of election is the sum of the Gospel, because of all words that can be said or heard it is the best: that God elects man; that God is for man too the One who loves in freedom'.[4] 'God took upon himself the condemna-tion of sinful men with all consequences, and elected men to participate in his eternal glory'.[5] This christological revision of the Reformed doctrine of predestination is the only way out of the old dilemma between Augustine and Pelagius, and the modern dilemma between fundamentalist evangelisations and a liberal disinterested tolerance of other religions.

Reformed 'according to the Word of God, attested in Holy Scripture'

This is the unique strength of Reformed theology, but fundamentalist biblicism is her weakness. Its dependence on a faithful exegesis of the Bible is certainly what Reformed theology must bring into the ecumenical dialogue. But we must fight against the misunderstanding of the Bible in fundamentalism. If we can't do this, who can? And fundamentalist belief in the verbal inspiration of the Scripture will grow in the near future, because people wish to have something to put their trust on in a world of many public and political lies.

Reformed theology didn't begin with Luther's fundamental differentiation of 'Law and Gospel.' Reformed theologians added to the reformatory '*sola scriptura*,' the formula '*tota scriptura*.' They understood the law (Torah) as a valid form of living before God and a promise for the coming kingdom. They understood the gospel not in contrast, but as fulfilment of the law, because in Christ all God's promises are yes and amen. Both the law and the gospel point beyond themselves to the coming kingdom of God. They stand therefore not in succession but side by side with their indications and expectations of God's future. For this reason Reformed theology has searched time and again for a unified 'biblical theology.' In my words: it has seen the canon within the canon, or the matter of scripture (*Die Sache der Schrift*), not in a 'centre of Scripture', but in the future of what 'is written.' Scripture points beyond itself to the *parousia* of Christ and the coming of God. This eschatological expectation makes it possible to read Scripture historically without burying it as past history, and it makes it possible to hear the promissory memory of Scripture today without idolizing it in a fundamentalist fashion. We need a new 'biblical theology' which keeps Old and New Testament together and is open for systematic and practical theology, and others can and should be able to expect this from the camp of Reformed theology.

I do not agree with Nobuo Watanabe, who wrote, 'The exegetical character of theology defines not only the method of investigation and treatment of the Church's doctrine but also theology's self-restriction to the revealed and written word of God.'[6] 'Revelation' is not a doctrine, once and for ever 'written down,' but is rather the self-revelation of the living God. God's Holy Spirit is inspiring us through God's Word, attested in Holy Scripture, but Scripture is not the prison of God's Spirit. Scripture is the prominent instrument of the world-renewing work of God the Holy Spirit. One should not say: 'Every doctrinal article is restricted to the content of Holy Scripture.'[7] Theology is more than the repetition of Bible quotations, it is the creative translation process of God's promise into new situations and new cultures. God's living Word is always and everywhere in context and *kairos* and community. It is not the idea of Scripture to become abstract, timeless and unrelated like the dogma according to Vicenz of Lerinum which is '*semper idem*,' infallible and irreformable.

The divine mystery of the earth

Critics of Reformed theology missed a doctrine of nature. Indeed, because Reformed theology was so close to the spirit of the modern age it has the typically modern anthropocentric characteristics of that age and was often solely concerned with the relationship between God and humankind rather than with the relationship between God and nature. And because it emphasized the transcendent sovereignty of God it was more interested in the 'demystification' and secularization of nature than in the immanent presence of God's Spirit in nature and thus the sanctification of the earth. Calvin however taught not only the transcendence of God over his creation as a 'work of his hands', but also the immanence of God's Spirit in every creature: 'For He is everywhere present and sustains, nourishes and enlivens all things in heaven and on earth.' (*Inst.*, 1.13.14). The eternal Spirit of the 'lover of life' is 'in all things', said the Hebrew Wisdom (12:1) and that the 'source of life' is 'poured out on all flesh', is the Pentecostal experience of God's presence. Compared with the Orthodox tradition, Reformed theology came late with this sacramental understanding of nature, but certainly not too late: in 1977 the World Alliance of Reformed Churches (WARC) published a 'Theological declaration on human rights' and in 1990 a declaration on the 'Rights of future generations and the rights of nature.' We are strong in terms of God's covenant with 'you, your descendents and all living beings' (Gen 9), but weak in a new cosmic spirituality which may bring humans into solidarity and friendship with the earth. We are still asking what we have to do now to nature: reconciliation with nature, liberation of nature, healing of nature, preservation of creation. We may not want to continue as the 'master and owner of nature' (Descartes); we want to do better as 'stewards of nature.' But would it not be best first of all to understand what in biblical terms the earth is as that which enables the 'bringing forth of the living creature' (Gen 1:24) and thus to respect the divine dignity of the earth as home and mother of all living beings? Should we humans then not become aware of the fact that we are latecomers on earth and must learn the wisdom of life from those beings who were here before us? Must we not first respect the responsibility the earth, in which we live, has taken for humankind and the gracious tolerance she has with us? How can we find our place and our destiny for the earth if we don't understand what the earth is doing in the name of the Creator to us? We may turn our sequence 'God–humankind–earth' around and balance it with the older sequence 'God–earth–humankind'. The first sequence we see working in the modern world and destroying nature, the second we find not only in the Chinese *Tao Te Ching*, but also in Psalm 104. The new cosmic spirituality must not be learned from the 'New Age movement.' We can also learn it from the cosmological christology in the letter to the Colossians. If 'by him were all things created ... and by him all things reconciled ...' (Col 1:16, 20), then there is a 'third mode of being' of Christ (Karl Barth): Christ in the cosmos. We find a good expression of this idea in Logion 77 of the Gospel of Thomas:

> Cleave the wood and I am there;
> Lift up a stone and there you shall find me.

We can open our eyes with Calvin and look around: 'Wherever you cast your eyes, there is not a spot in the universe wherein you cannot discern at least some sparks of his glory.' 'But', lamented Calvin, 'it is in vain that so many burning lamps shine for us ... Although they bathe us wholly in their radiance ... we have not the eyes to see ...' (*Inst.*, 1.51.68).

Can we now say that this is recognized – that the awe of God includes in itself the 'awe of life'? The love of God included in itself the love of the earth. The sanctification of human life includes therefore the sanctification of the earth. The friends of Christ are then the 'friends of the earth' as well.

Reformed theology must become a new reformatory theology at this point today and search for ecological justice after it has searched for economic justice and political justice in accord with the justice of God.

Notes

1 In discussion Professor Moltmann acknowledged that there were other churches so named, such as the 'Wesleyan Methodists' for example – but these were not normally Reformed churches.

2 Choan-Seng Song, "Christian Theology: Toward an Asian Reconstruction," in *Toward the Future of Reformed Theology* (ed. D. Willis and M. Welker; Grand Rapids: Wm. B. Eerdmanns, 1999), 64.

3 *The Mystery of Salvation: The Story of God's Gift; A Report by the Doctrine Commission of the General Synod of the Church of England* (London: Church House Publishing, 1995), 199.

4 Karl Barth, *Church Dogmatics*, II/2 (trans. G. W. Bromiley and T. F. Torrance; Edinburgh: T. & T. Clark, 1957), § 32, p. 3.

5 *Ibid.*, § 33, p. 94.

6 Nobuo Watanabe, "Reformed Theology in East and West," in Willis and Welker, *Toward the Future of Reformed Theology*, 43.

7 *Ibid.*

2

CONSTRUCTING TRADITION:
Schleiermacher, Hodge, and the
Theological Legacy of Calvin

B. A. GERRISH

I have offspring by the thousands all over Christendom.

–CALVIN

On 25 April 1564, shortly before his death, Calvin dictated his last will and testament to a Genevan notary, who certified that the Reformer, though sick in body, was of a sound mind. Calvin first reaffirmed his faith in the gospel: he had no other refuge, he said, than God's gratuitous adoption, on which alone his salvation depended. He then went on to specify how his slender patrimony was to be assigned. The boys' school, the fund for impoverished aliens, and the daughter of Calvin's half-sister, Marie, were each to receive ten crowns (*escus*). Next, Calvin designated unequal sums of money for the children born from his brother Antoine's two marriages: for two of the boys forty crowns each, for the three girls thirty each, and for their brother David only twenty-five, to chastise him for his frivolousness. Calvin added the proviso that should the sale of his books and other personal effects raise a larger amount than he expected, the surplus was to be distributed equally among the children – including David, 'if through the goodness of God he had returned to good behaviour.'[1] The testator thus exercised full control over his legacy, discriminating as he saw fit among his several beneficiaries: the girls received less than two of the boys, but David received less than the girls. Though Calvin would not be in a position to supervise the way the children spent their inheritance, he alone determined how much each of them had to spend.

Quite different from a monetary bequest is a theological legacy. It is not only possible for Calvin's theological heirs to spend their inheritance in ways he might not approve: even what they receive is pretty much what they decide to take. In this sense, a Calvinist tradition is not simply a bequest but a construct – something we make rather than passively receive.[2] Bickering over the inheritance is likely. Not that everyone will want the same things from the treasure chest; the argument will be over the value of the things chosen. There are certainly limits to what one may reasonably claim as Calvin's theological legacy. It is always possible to protest, 'Calvin never said that,' or, 'That's not what he meant,' or, 'Well, he did say that, but it's not all he said.' Still, appropriating Calvin's theological legacy is not the same as getting him right, or setting the historical record straight: the difference between his time and ours makes it impossible to take him just as he was, and we are deluding ourselves if we think otherwise. An appeal to Calvin's legacy as a theological warrant, even if it presupposes historical knowledge, is not a historical procedure. What he said may have a certain prima facie weight among those who locate themselves in a Calvinist tradition. For the theologian, however, the appeal to Calvin must be subjected to the same theological norms as everything else. The pre-eminent norm will naturally be the one to which he himself pointed his readers in the preface to the 1541 French *Institutes*: 'Above all, they will be well advised to resort to Scripture, in order to ponder the testimonies I advance from it.'[3] And precisely because our time is not his time, most theologians will recognise in the present state of knowledge outside the Scriptures a second norm, whether as part of a full-blown method of correlation or simply in recognition of the need to adapt and apply whatever we receive from the past.

It is not my intention in this essay to make a case either for or against Calvin's legacy, or any part of it. For now, I am interested in a third task that falls between determining what his theology was and appropriating his theology today: I mean the quest for examples of how Calvin's theological legacy has, as a matter of fact, been perceived or assimilated by others in other times. The quest may well be undertaken for the sake of the properly theological task, but it is itself strictly historical. Obviously, there is more than enough material out there to fill an entire book on the reception of Calvin's theological legacy from the sixteenth to the twentieth century. I am not aware of any attempt to write such a comprehensive study. If the attempt were made, the result would not be just a history of Calvin scholarship, and it would not be a book quite like McNeill's classic *History and Character of Calvinism*, in which the precise connection of Calvinism with Calvin is not the focus of inquiry.[4] Neither, incidentally, would it be a book like Bornkamm's *Luther im Spiegel der deutschen Geistesgeschichte*, which traces the changing images of Martin Luther reflected in the successive phases of German intellectual history.[5] The eagerness of the Germans to claim Luther's authority for their various programs has made him the patron of an astonishing number of mutually exclusive causes. The Reformed, by contrast, despite one or two attempts at hagiography, have not discovered in John Calvin good material for a personality cult, and in modern times they have not always turned instinctively to his theology as the touchstone of pure doctrine. But at no time has he been without his beneficiaries, and for now I want to think about just two of them: Friedrich Schleiermacher (1768–1834) and Charles Hodge (1797–1878). Then I will offer one or two concluding comments about Calvin's theological legacy. To anticipate: I want to show, first, that Schleiermacher and Hodge exemplify two quite different views of faithfulness to a tradition and, second, that Schleiermacher's view bears a striking resemblance to Calvin's understanding of Luther and the Reformation tradition.

Schleiermacher was the greatest theologian of the Reformed church between Calvin and Barth. Only Jonathan Edwards comes close. I have made more than one previous attempt to explore the question of Schleiermacher's relation to Luther, the Reformation, and especially Calvin, always concluding that much more needs to be done.[6] The most obvious reason for neglect of the question is that since the 1920s the canonical narrative of Protestant history has represented Schleiermacher's thought as a disastrous break with the heritage of the Reformation. Karl Barth's famous declaration of 1922 set the pattern. Speaking of the line that runs back through Kierkegaard to Luther and Calvin, and so to Paul and Jeremiah, Barth added: 'And to be absolutely clear, I would like to point out expressly that in the ancestral line I am commending to you the name Schleiermacher does not appear.'[7] The most detailed and comprehensive critique of Schleiermacher from what we commonly call the 'neo-orthodox' camp was written not by Barth, but by his associate Emil Brunner. In *Die Mystik und das Wort* (1924), Brunner passionately accused his adversary of replacing biblical-Reformation faith with a mystical religion; taking this hermeneutic key in hand, he exposed the alleged flaws in a wide range of Schleiermacher's doctrines.[8] A few years later, an article by Wilhelm Niesel dealt specifically with Schleiermacher's relation to the Reformed tradition. His negative conclusion was stated as an ironical

question: Did Schleiermacher's supposedly Reformed makeup consist only
in the fact that he possessed a Reformed certificate of baptism?[9]

Brunner and Niesel considered the matter closed; Barth was never quite
so sure.[10] But it must be added that the way the neo-orthodox theologians
construed the story found some support from German historians, who
professed disappointment with Schleiermacher's strange failure to display
much warmth in speaking of Martin Luther.[11] And here one must note another
reason for the state of the secondary literature: in Germany the assumption
– sometimes tacit, sometimes spoken – has always been that the Reformation
means Luther. Hence the question of Schleiermacher's connection with the
Reformation is presumed to have been answered when his rare and somewhat
restrained remarks about Luther have been duly noted and lamented. But the
obvious next step would be to see if he spoke more approvingly either of the
Reformation in general or of John Calvin in particular, the reformer most
esteemed in Schleiermacher's own church. Though German, Schleiermacher
was not a Lutheran, and even after the union of the Lutherans and the
Reformed in 1817, which he supported, he continued to profess his allegiance
to what he called 'the Reformed school.'[12]

It must be said, to begin with, that one should not expect much more
warmth in Schleiermacher's references to Calvin than in his references to
Luther. He understood history to be everywhere the collective work of a
'common spirit' and was unwilling to attribute too much to individuals.[13] He
hoped that when the dividing names 'Lutheran' and 'Reformed' disappeared
in the Church of the Union, it would no longer seem as if the Reformed were
less respectful than the Lutherans of the man after whom the Lutherans were
named, nor yet as if the Lutherans were less concerned than the Reformed to
avoid glorifying any one man too much.[14] He viewed Luther's achievement
as part of a larger, unfinished Reformation that could not be the work of
any single individual, but in which several individuals – Erasmus, Luther,
Zwingli, Calvin, and others – have all played their essential roles.[15] No
belittling of any one of them, nor of the Reformation itself, was intended.
Schleiermacher believed that he still lived and did his theology in the period
of the Reformation, which was likely to endure for a good many more years:
no comparable epoch separated him from the first generation of Protestants.[16]
For the Reformation was not merely a correction of abuses; much less was
it simply the restitution of the apostolic age. It brought into existence a new
and distinctive formation of the Christian spirit, which for the foreseeable

future would stand over against the Catholic type of Christianity.[17] The work of theology, or more exactly the work of dogmatic theology, had to be determined by the 'antithesis' of Catholic and Protestant. Schleiermacher had more than one way of defining the exact nature of the antithesis. Sometimes he located it in the contrast between symbolic action and the word; sometimes in the different ways the two communions represent the relation of the individual to the church.[18] But, for now, there is no need to examine the content he assigned to the confessional antithesis. The point is simply that if we are to understand his references to Calvin, we have to read them in the context of what he made of the Protestant Reformation. Then we will not be disappointed if we find little inclination to venerate Calvin, or even to elevate him above the other evangelical Reformers.

This leads me to a second contextual point, closely related to the first. If the Reformation is the collective work of a common spirit, collective expressions of the Reformation will naturally be assigned dogmatic precedence over the opinions of individual theologians. With this in mind, no one need be surprised that Schleiermacher's great dogmatic work, *The Christian Faith* (2nd ed., 1830–31), especially the second part, bristles with quotations from the Protestant confessions; often, he introduces a new theme with a long catena of passages. At the time of his writing, the authority of so-called symbolic books was the centre of a heated theological controversy, in which he was obliged more than once to take a public stand. Ironically, the formation of the united church coincided with the rise of Lutheran confessionalism and even intensified it. Many Lutherans feared that association with the Reformed might further dilute the purity of Lutheranism, already threatened by rationalism, and they called for strict adherence to their Reformation creeds. In response, Schleiermacher pointed to a middle way between rationalism and inflexible confessionalism. He professed astonishment that there were those who would have erased so many years of church history, demanding subscription to a document from the sixteenth century. But if this set him firmly against the Lutheran confessionalists, it did not align him with the opposing rationalist party, which held that precisely because the Reformation confessions were written for their own time, they were mere historical documents and had no claim to present-day attention. This view too in its own way, he argued, betrayed a lack of historical sense. For there is always a difference between the first decisive moments and the subsequent course of a historical phenomenon, and between a merely personal statement and one that represents a widespread conviction. Although we are not forever bound to the letter, the confessions have their unique worth as the first public expressions of the Protestant spirit, which is identical in both the Lutheran and the Reformed churches.[19] The difference between the two communions that trace their lineage back to the Reformation is only a difference of 'school': not, that is, a divergence in the religious affections, but in the way they are represented.[20]

It is against the background of these fundamental principles that Schleiermacher's attitude to Calvin and his theological legacy is to be understood. He could not confer on Calvin the value reserved for the Reformation confessions, both Lutheran and Reformed, and he was not tempted to make him a denominational hero. Within these limits, his judgements on Calvin are generous. He did not claim to be a Calvin scholar with a broad knowledge of the *Opera Omnia*, but he was well acquainted with the *Institutes*. When a theological opponent attributed a dubious sentiment to Calvin, Schleiermacher's reaction was confident: 'I cannot find this principle anywhere in my Calvin; rather, as I consider the matter more closely, I find grounds enough in my slight knowledge of Calvin to assert that he cannot have written that.' The expression 'my Calvin' is intriguing. By his 'slight knowledge of Calvin' he evidently meant his limited acquaintance with other works of Calvin besides the *Institutes*. For when the opponent supplied a reference, it turned out that he had misrepresented a passage on election from the third book of the *Institutes*, with which Schieiermacher was perfectly well acquainted. 'And I thought the proof would come,' he remarks, 'from who knows what more seldom read commentary of Calvin!'[21] We can safely infer that he had not spent much time reading Calvin's commentaries. But he seems to have been at home in the *Institutes*, which he admired for two main reasons. First, he judged it a priceless work because it never loses touch with the religious affections, not even in the most intricate material. Second, it is distinguished by sharpness of method and systematic compass.[22] Though he regretted the fact that in Calvin the systematic impulse was hindered by a polemical tendency, it is obvious that Schleiermacher admired most in the *Institutes* exactly what he himself strove for in his own systematic work, *The Christian Faith*.[23] But it does not necessarily follow that he actually owed his methodological ideals to Calvin's theological legacy. The next question is whether he was indebted to Calvin for the content he gave to some of his dogmatic themes.

There are a number of points at which a comparison between the 1559 *Institutes* and the second edition of *The Christian Faith* proves very interesting. Some of them I have taken up elsewhere.[24] But resemblances, if and when they emerge, do not establish debts; and the comparison just as often uncovers differences, whether or not they reflect conscious modifications or corrections of the Calvinist heritage. For this reason, I want to confine my attention to the passages in *The Christian Faith* in which Calvin is expressly named. There are sixteen references to Calvin[25] – more than to Zwingli (7) or Luther (13), but fewer than the references to Johann Gerhard (19), Melanchthon (21), Reinhard (25), or Augustine (33). Obviously, I cannot take a close look at all Schleiermacher's Calvin citations, but I can at least make a start. All the references, without exception, are to the *Institutes*: six to book 1, two to book 2, five to book 3, and three to book 4. It is not always certain whether Calvin is being cited to confirm Schleiermacher's argument, or to exemplify a position he is criticising. He tells us, for instance, it is questionable (*bedenklich*) to teach that angels bring outside protection to us, and he adds a footnote reference to the *Institutes*.[26] Now, in the place cited Calvin does assert that angels are our protectors, though he hesitates to say that each of us has a personal guardian angel; but he warns us against transferring to the angels what belongs to God and Christ.[27] So, is he cited disapprovingly for his assertion, or approvingly for his warning? Perhaps both, since Schleiermacher thinks the hazard is great enough to warrant the complete exclusion of angel talk from dogmatics, allowing it only a limited private and liturgical use.[28] Similarly ambivalent is a passage in which Calvin is described as acute (*scharfsinnig*), but unable to put together a consistent account of the Devil's activity from the different strands in the biblical allusions to him.[29]

Schleiermacher can of course quote what Calvin says, without either endorsing or criticising it, simply as one of the views held on the theme under discussion. This is the point of his quotations from Calvin on the Lord's Supper: we have to distinguish the Lutheran, the Zwinglian, and the Calvinistic views, but none of them is free from difficulties.[30] Mostly, however, he refers to Calvin to indicate their agreement. The list of approving references is interesting. Calvin's reading of the Mosaic creation narrative rules out the use of Genesis to construct an actual theory of creation. Calvin asserted that God foresees future events because he decreed them. (A good point, Schleiermacher thinks, but John Scotus Erigena [810–77] put it better when he said 'God sees', not 'God foresees', what he willed to make.) Again, Calvin refused to say that the contagion of original sin is transmitted through the substance of either the flesh or the soul. He rightly distinguished God's will from his precept (that is, the efficient from the commanding will of God). Whereas some deny the necessity for the baptised to be converted, Calvin represented baptism precisely as the 'seed' of future repentance and faith. And he held it to be beyond controversy that no-one is loved by God outside of Christ.[31] On all of these six points, then, Calvin gives expression to thoughts that Schleiermacher shares with him. He is drawing on the theological legacy of Calvin – whether to confirm his own thoughts or to acknowledge a formative influence on them is hard to say. But I have saved until last the most instructive of his attempts to see himself in Calvin's lineage: his adherence to the doctrine of election, which led his contemporaries to characterise him as a 'bold and resolute disciple of Calvin.'

Schleiermacher defended election in the long, 119-page article that launched the *Theologische Zeitschrift* in 1819.[32] He stated expressly that he wished to take up the doctrine in its original presentation in Calvin's *Institutes*, avoiding the later Canons of Dort (1618–19). The argument of the article is carried over into *The Christian Faith*, only there, as one would expect, in the form not of an apology for Calvin but of a constructive statement, followed as usual by an assessment of the official church teachings (*kirchliche Lehrsätze*). Schleiermacher's key thought is very simple: The kingdom of God established by Christ is a phenomenon of history, and it is therefore impossible that the whole of humanity should be taken into it at one time. What proceeds from a single point can spread only gradually. This 'law' is so plainly a part of the divine governance of the world that we must judge the antithesis between those who are, and those who are not, members of the Church to be grounded solely in the divine good-pleasure. But it is a vanishing antithesis as Christianity spreads, and the Christian consciousness cannot suppose that because some die outside the kingdom, a part of the human race is intended to be finally excluded. In other words, we hope for the antithesis to continue diminishing even after death.[33]

It is when he turns to the ecclesiastical doctrines that Schleiermacher refers to Calvin. Like him, he has been wrestling with the evident inequality in the operations of grace; and like him he can attribute it only to the divine good-pleasure. Now he quotes Calvin directly three times, but each time with a critical comment or in a context that, in part, runs counter to Calvin's views. (1) Calvin says that election could not stand unless set over against reprobation. Schleiermacher agrees, but only in the limited sense that those who at any particular time are passed over or rejected are not yet chosen. We have no warrant for concluding that they never will be.[34] (2) Calvin speaks of a twofold foreordination, either to blessedness or to damnation. Schleiermacher argues that there is but one divine foreordination – the decree to assume the human race into fellowship with Christ.[35] (3) Calvin defines predestination as the eternal decree of God by which he determined what he willed to become of each individual. Schleiermacher protests against any atomistic view of the work of redemption and understands the operations of grace on the individual strictly in relation to the one eternal decree to redeem humanity in Christ.[36] So, was Schleiermacher a 'bold and resolute disciple of Calvin' or not? I shall come back to the question in my conclusion. But first some reflections on Charles Hodge. They will need to be much briefer.

Hodge was not an original thinker of Schleiermacher's calibre, but he was surely the greatest American Calvinist since Jonathan Edwards (1703– 58).[37] Not a Calvin scholar, as B. B. Warfield (1851–1921) was a little later at Princeton, he was a learned advocate of the Calvinist theological legacy – or, as he often said, 'the Augustinian system.' He was appalled at the direction German theology had taken, partly under the lead of Schleiermacher's charismatic personality. In a way, his critical estimate of Schleiermacher anticipated Brunner's, since it ended in a perplexing conflict between the two sides of the father of modern theology: his devout faith in Christ and his allegedly pagan philosophy.[38] Hodge reached back into the seventeenth century for sounder and safer theological models. With a sigh of relief, he wrote: 'After all the alleged improvements in theological research, we never feel so much disposed to take down one of the old Latin dogmatic writers of the seventeenth century, as immediately on closing a fresh work from Germany.'[39] Our question must be, then, whether by way of Francis Turretin (1623–87) and the other orthodox divines Hodge received a larger bequest from Calvin than Schleiermacher did. Different it was certain to be. Schleiermacher held that theological progress, though it cannot be heretical, is bound to be heterodox and must include an honest critique of the official dogmas of the Church.[40] Hodge, by contrast, liked to commend his opinions as biblical and orthodox – nothing more than the Church had always taught.[41] Interestingly, there was at least one topic on which he had to locate Schleiermacher closer than himself to Johann Gerhard (1582–

1637) and Johann Heinrich Heidegger (1633–98). He conceded that for the seventeenth-century theologians, both Lutheran and Reformed, the divine 'simplicity' made it impossible to allow any real distinctions between one divine attribute and another, and he recognized that this put Schleiermacher in the succession of the orthodox divines, whereas he himself wanted to take the distinctions between God's various attributes in Scripture at face value.[42] But this odd change of dancing partners did not lead him to have second thoughts about Schleiermacher's relation to the dogmatic tradition.

When it comes to direct references to Calvin, Hodge easily out-quotes Schleiermacher. The index to the three-volume *Systematic Theology* (1871–72) directs us to twenty-eight places where Calvin is named or quoted, in one of which multiple pages in the third volume are indicated.[43] In some of the places mentioned, more than one actual citation from Calvin is given; in two, there are excursuses headed 'Calvin's Doctrine' (on justification and the Lord's Supper). The total number of citations also needs to be adjusted to allow for the fact that Hodge quotes the Geneva Catechism (1545) without assigning it to Calvin's authorship and, conversely, cites the *Consensus Tigurinus* (1549; published 1551) as though Calvin were its sole author. Further, the index is not complete.[44] But I am not anxious to determine Hodge's exact score, so to say. The point is to discern the pattern in his references to Calvin. Let me make three observations.

First, most of the references are to the 1559 *Institutes*, but not all. Hodge also quotes from Calvin's *Harmony of the Gospels* (on Matt 19:10–11); from the commentaries on Romans, 1 Timothy, and Titus; and from the Geneva Catechism, the Scholars' Confession (1559), the treatise against Tileman Heshusius (1561), and two of Calvin's letters.[45] Three quotations from Calvin are given without identification of their sources.[46] Clearly, Hodge had some acquaintance with the commentaries and other 'who knows what more seldom read' writings of Calvin.

Second, as we would expect, nearly all the discussions of Calvin serve as corroboration for Hodge's own views, but again not all. Aside from the place where Hodge simply notes that Calvin used the word 'regeneration' more inclusively than ourselves, to denote the entire Christian life and not just its beginning,[47] he differs with Calvin on two topics: on virginity and on what he calls 'the peculiar views of Calvin' on the Lord's Supper.[48] I will come back to the Lord's Supper in a moment. Hodge is surprisingly vehement in his critique of the views on virginity and marriage in book two of the

Institutes (*Inst.*, 2.8.41–42, the only passage he refers to in the second book). He comments: '[Calvin says that] virginity is a virtue. Celibacy is a higher state than marriage. Those who cannot live in that state should descend to the lower platform of married life. With such dregs of Manichean philosophy was the pure truth of the Bible contaminated even as held by the most illustrious Reformers.'[49] Hodge does not mention that Calvin was attempting an honest interpretation of the Lord's saying about men who castrate themselves for the sake of the kingdom (Matt 19:12) and Paul's unsentimental view of marriage as a divine remedy for lust (1 Cor 7:2). Calvin's assertion that nature and the fall combine to make us 'doubly subject to women's society' does make you wonder about him, but it may not be necessary to explain it by 'the dregs of Manichean philosophy'.

This brings me to my third observation: Though he quotes Calvin often, Hodge's use of Calvin, whether approving or disapproving, is not always fair. On the whole, I think, he is honest enough. But sometimes he selects only what he wants (don't we all?), and sometimes he twists the evidence (we don't do that). It is remarkable that in his long argument against baptismal regeneration Hodge's only quotation from Calvin is a bland remark retrieved from his Commentary on Titus 3:5, '*Partam a Christo salutem baptismus nobis obsignat.*'[50] Hodge says nothing of Calvin's argument in the *Institutes* that God can, and sometimes certainly does, effect the regeneration of baptised infants.[51] On the other evangelical sacrament, Hodge seems in one place clearly to misuse the sources. He concedes that Calvin spoke of receiving a supernatural power that flows from Christ's life-giving flesh in heaven. But he repudiates this 'peculiar' notion and tries to show that it was only a minor strand, not only in Reformed theology generally, but even in Calvin's own thoughts on the Lord's Supper. Calvin, he says, 'avowed his agreement with Zwingli [sic] and Oecolampadius on all questions related to the sacraments.' However, 'at times' he did teach the peculiar notion of an influence from the glorified body of Christ. As evidence, Hodge quotes from Calvin's exposition of the *Consensus Tigurinus*. 'Unless,' he goes on, 'we are willing to accuse the illustrious Calvin of inconsistency, his meaning must be made to harmonise with what he says elsewhere.' And to prove his point, Hodge quotes from the *Consensus* itself.[52] But this, surely, is to get things exactly the wrong way around. Calvin wrote the *Expositio* as a fuller explanation of the *Consensus*, fearing that its brevity might leave it vulnerable to quibbling. If there is some tension between the explanation and the document itself, we should attribute it not only to the brevity of the *Consensus*, but also to its character as a compromise document, in which Calvin did not say all he liked to say about the Lord's Supper. His *Expositio* is where we must look to find out what was in his mind during the negotiations. An *expositio* by the co-author of the *Consensus*, Heinrich Bullinger (1504–75), would no doubt look very different.[53]

Hodge's fascinating debate on the Lord's Supper with John Williamson Nevin (1803–86) was an immensely instructive chapter in the history of Calvin's theological legacy. I have written about it elsewhere and do not want to delay too much over it here, other than to reaffirm its importance to our present topic.[54] It was a clash between two varieties of Calvinism, the one predestinarian and the other sacramental. Hodge had no antenna for Calvin's strange talk about the life-giving flesh of Christ. He could not deny that Calvin did talk that way ('at times'!), but he explained that this was an 'uncongenial foreign element' in Reformed theology, partly derived from Lutheran influence, and he did not wish to be troubled with the 'private authority of Calvin.'[55] For his part, Nevin was convinced that Calvin's talk of Christ's life-giving flesh was all-important, not least because it excluded the Zwinglian alternative. He admitted, however, that much of Calvin's language was fantastic and tried to re-clothe the substance of it in modern categories – leaving him open to Hodge's accusation that he had fallen victim to the dreaded German philosophy.[56] Moreover, Nevin was convinced that there is a fundamental disharmony between Calvin's predestinarianism and his sacramentalism, and that increasing obsession with the divine decrees was responsible for the decline of the authentic Calvinistic view of the Eucharist.[57] If Hodge ceded Calvin's eucharistic theology to Mercersburg, then, Nevin gladly let Princeton keep the Calvin of the 'horrible decree'.

Nevin was a learned adversary. James Hastings Nichols, the historian of the Mercersburg theology, suspected that Hodge's Calvin citations were actually gleaned from Nevin's copious footnotes, and he concluded that Hodge was 'beyond his depth ... He made the mistake of challenging a man whose command of the field was vastly greater than his own.'[58] Personally, I would distribute the honours a bit more evenly. Hodge rightly challenged Nevin's belief that in the Calvinistic Eucharist there is 'an altogether extraordinary power,' quite different from what is available in the preached word. Nevin (like Schleiermacher) understood the Calvinistic doctrine to assert a real presence of Christ's body and blood in the Supper not available anywhere else. Hodge had no difficulty showing that, as an interpretation of Calvin, this was a mistake.[59]

Hodge's debate with Nevin was partly a difference over the interpretation of Calvin, partly a difference over what there is in his legacy that is worth preserving. In short, it was consciously, directly, and expressly an *argument* about the theology of Calvin: what it was and where it was sound. I want to end my remarks on Hodge and the Calvinist tradition by commenting briefly on a paradigmatic issue of another kind, in which the question is not directly about Calvin, but about an *uncontroverted* theological concept that can be traced back to him. The schema of the *munus triplex* – Christ's three offices as prophet, priest, and king – had become an accepted resource in the theologian's equipment for interpreting the work of Christ. Calvin is credited with introducing it into Protestant dogmatics, though he himself did not make as much use of it as he leads us to expect.[60] In book two of the *Institutes*, the fifteenth chapter sets up the framework. We are to look at three things in Christ: his 'offices' as prophet, king, and priest. Calvin takes the offices to denote not only a work of Christ accomplished *extra nos*, but also an activity into which believers are drawn along with him. But chapter 16 appears to leave the threefold office behind and to concentrate heavily, if not quite exclusively, on the priestly work of Christ on our behalf.

Similarly, Hodge begins his discussion of the work of Christ with the threefold office of the Mediator, and he stresses its dogmatic importance:

> We as fallen men, ignorant, guilty, polluted, and helpless, need a Saviour who is a prophet to instruct us; a priest to atone and to make intercession for us; and a king to rule over and protect us ... This is not, therefore, simply a convenient classification of the contents of his mission and work, but it enters into its very nature, and must be retained in our theology if we would take the truth as it is revealed in the Word of God.[61]

But Hodge develops the *munus triplex* even less than Calvin did, and his rearrangement of the sequence – now prophet, priest, and king – makes the imbalance in his treatment of the offices very obvious. The presentation of the priestly office is so long that the reader has probably forgotten the kingly office by the time it receives its short chapter. Hodge's discussion of the work of Christ runs to 184 pages. He needs but two pages to dispose of the prophetic office, and only a slightly more generous fourteen to explain the kingly office. In between he lingers for no fewer than 132 pages over Christ's priestly work, most of them on the idea of satisfaction for sin (128 pages), but with a short addition (four pages) on Christ's priestly intercession. Further, Hodge takes the work of the Mediator to be a work performed strictly *extra nos* – outside of ourselves, in our place, in our stead. Calvin's notion of a threefold work of Christ performed both *for* us and *in* us is conspicuously absent.

Now, the striking absence of balance in Hodge's treatment of the three offices and his one-sided emphasis on the work of Christ in our place could, of course, reflect a sound grasp of dogmatic priorities. It would require a move from the historical to the dogmatic mode if I wished to pronounce a theological verdict on what Hodge does here – or does not do – with the tradition. I am certainly not shy about making such a move in the proper place. But let me, for now, simply conclude my remarks on Hodge with a comparison. When Schleiermacher comes to speak of the ecclesiastical doctrine of the Redeemer's threefold office, he commends it precisely because it prevents undue emphasis on a single aspect of Christ's redeeming and reconciling activity, and he is closer than Hodge to Calvin's understanding of the entire work of Christ as, at least in part, an activity into which Christians are drawn by and with Christ.[62] Schleiermacher makes no reference to Calvin's treatment of the threefold office. Neither does Hodge. Had he done so, he might have had second thoughts about both his and Schleiermacher's interpretations of the work of Christ. Evidently, one of the ways in which Calvin's offspring may relate to his legacy is by way of oversight or neglect – unwitting failure to explore further what Calvin left simply in the form of hints and possibilities.

When a mean-spirited adversary, Francois Baudouin, made a joke of Calvin's childlessness, Calvin replied that he had offspring by thousands all over Christendom.[63] So he did – and still does. But his heirs have not all used his legacy in the same measure or the same way. Sometimes they seem to have drawn unconsciously on their heritage, or equally unconsciously to have neglected it. But they have also argued over what Calvin said, what he meant, and what he left that is worth preserving. From the two examples I have given it is, I think, plain that the way the legacy is used is determined in part by fundamental dogmatic principles. Hodge, on the whole, held a static view of past sources and norms. True, I was able to point to one place in which he notes that a dogmatic term, 'regeneration,' is differently employed by us today than in his day by Calvin. But he does not stop to ask if the change of term reflects a change of thought. In this instance, it probably doesn't. And in general the question did not arise at all for Hodge, who understood the language of the theological tradition, like the language of Scripture, to be immobile. Hence, when reading Calvin, he could agree with what he read, or (less often) he could disagree; there was no third option. And the criterion of 'orthodoxy,' by which he judged even Calvin, meant firm adherence to what the Church had always believed and taught as the sense of Scripture.[64]

Schleiermacher held a quite different, developmental understanding of tradition. This is nowhere more clear than in his doctrine of election. He did not quote passages from Calvin on the subject simply in order to agree with some, disagree with others. Rather, he wrestled with the idea of election, thought he saw what was important in Calvin's treatment of it, and tried to formulate it anew. As for Calvin's actual language, he could appropriate some of his terms, limit the application of others, and quietly set yet others aside. Had he persuaded his church to follow him in his admittedly heterodox moves, then the single divine decree that creates only a vanishing, temporal division in the human race would have become orthodox; for orthodoxy, as Schleiermacher understood it, was not what the church had always and everywhere taught, but what had become the prevailing doctrine in a particular church at a particular time.[65]

So was Schleiermacher a 'bold and resolute disciple of Calvin'? If we think of the disciple as one who simply echoes the words of the master, our answer will be 'No.' But an interesting fact is worth mentioning when Calvin's theological legacy is under discussion. To those who refused to move beyond the details of Martin Luther's eucharistic teaching Calvin observed, with his customary tact, that there is a difference between a disciple and an ape.[66] To one of his correspondents he wrote: 'If I was not permitted at any point to depart from the opinion of Luther, it was utterly ridiculous of me to undertake the office of interpretation (*munus interpretandi*).'[67] Similarly, when accused by Albert Pighius (c. 1490–1542) of diverging from Luther's opinions on free will, Calvin replied, 'If Pighius does not know it, I want to make this plain to him: our constant endeavour, day and night, is to form in the manner we think will be best whatever is faithfully handed on by us.'[68] *Fideliter tradere* is also *formare*. There is an affinity between Schleiermacher's use of Calvin and Calvin's use of Luther. We might even venture to say that we find in them both something like the old motto *Ecclesia reformata, semper reformanda*. But it is not an easy conception of the theological task to put into practice. If the obvious difficulty with Hodge's appeal to two thirds of the Vincentian canon (*Quodsemper, quod ubique*) is that it is only a pious fantasy, the idea of a developing tradition poses acutely the problem of continuity. For did Calvin leave the substance of Luther's opinions unchanged, as he believed, merely expressing them more judiciously? Ask any Lutheran. And was Schleiermacher really the champion of Calvin and his doctrine of election, or was he proposing a new doctrine? If his doctrine of election was something new, shall we call it a development or apostasy?[69] I hope I may have taken a small step toward answering these questions by showing that traditions are not simply given but constructed; and that when we look for continuity, we need to ask ourselves what kind of continuity we seek – Hodge's or Schleiermacher's, the preservation of past doctrines or development of them.[70]

Notes

1   Calvin's will is reproduced in French in *Joannis Calvini opera quae supersunt omnia* (hereafter *CO*), eds. Wilhelm Baum, Eduard Cunitz, and Eduard Reuss, 59 vols., Corpus reformatorum, vols. 29–87 (Brunswick: C. A. Schwetschke & Son [M. Bruhn], 1863–1900), 20:298–302. It is also given in Latin in the third version of Beza's life of Calvin: Theodore Beza, *Ioannis Calvini vita* (1575), *CO*, 21:162–64.

2   Strictly speaking, Calvin's theological 'legacy' is the *Opera omnia*. It is what is *taken* from this legacy that constitutes a theological 'tradition'.

3   *Institution de la religion chrestienne* (1541), "Argument du présent livre," in *Joannis Calvini opera selecta* (hereafter *OS*), eds. Peter Barth, Wilhelm Niesel, and Doris Scheuner, 5 vols. (Munich: Chr. Kaiser Verlag, 1926–52), 3:8. Trans. mine.

4   John T. McNeill, *The History and Character of Calvinism* (New York: Oxford University Press, 1954).

5   Heinrich Bornkamm, *Luther im Spiegel der deutschen Geistesgeschichte, mit ausgewählten Texten von Lessing bis zur Gegenwart* (Heidelberg: Quelle & Meyer, 1955).

6   See especially "Schleiermacher and the Reformation: A Question of Doctrinal Development" (1980), reprinted in B. A. Gerrish, *The Old Protestantism and the New: Essays on the Reformation Heritage* (Chicago: University of Chicago Press; Edinburgh: T. & T. Clark, 1982), chap. 11, and "From Calvin to Schleiermacher:

The Theme and the Shape of Christian Dogmatics" (1985), reprinted in B. A. Gerrish, *Continuing the Reformation: Essays on Modern Religious Thought* (Chicago: University of Chicago Press, 1993), chap. 8.

7 Karl Barth, "Das Wort Gottes als Aufgabe der Theologie" (1922), *Karl Barth Gesamtausgabe,* 3,19 (Zurich: Theologischer Verlag, 1990), 158. Barth's emphasis; my trans.

8 [H.] Emil Brunner, *Die Mystik und das Wort: Der Gegensatz zwischen moderner Religionsauffassung und christlichem Glauben dargestellt an der Theologie Schleiermachers* (Tübingen: J. C. B. Mohr [Paul Siebeck], 1924; 2nd ed., 1928).

9 Wilhelm Niesel, "Schleiermachers Verhältnis zur reformierten Tradition," in *Zwischen den Zeiten* 8 (1930): 511–25.

10 See Barth's review of Brunner's *Die Mystik und das Wort*: "Brunners Schleiermacherbuch," *Zwischen den Zeiten* 2 (1924): 49–64, p. 60. The apparent uncertainty – despite some heady rhetoric – continued to the year of Barth's death, when he admitted he was not so sure of his own cause that his 'yes' entailed a 'no' to Schleiermacher's cause. Heinz Bolli, ed., *Schleiermacher – Auswahl mit einem Nachwort von Karl Barth* (Munich and Hamburg: Siebenstern Taschenbuch Verlag, 1968), 307.

11 I mentioned some of the pertinent literature in the articles referred to in n. 6 above.

12 See, for example, Schleiermacher, *An Herrn Oberhofprediger Dr. Ammon über seine Prüfung der Harmsischen Säze* (1818), in *Friedrich Schleiermachers sämmtliche Werke* (hereafter *SW,* cited by division, volume, and page), 31 vols. (Berlin: Georg Reimer, 1834–64), 1,5:341.

13 He applies this view of history expressly to the Reformation in *Geschichte der christlichen Kirche, aus Schleiermachers handschriftlichem Nachlasse und nachgeschriebenen Vorlesungen herausgegeben* (1840), *SW,* 1,11:576.

14 *An Ammon, SW,* 1,5:396–97.

15 Besides the references in nn. 13 and 14, see *Geschichte der Kirche, SW,* 1,11:582–83 (on the role of Erasmus).

16 *Kurze Darstellung des theologischen Studiums zum Behuf einleitender Vorlesungen* (hereafter *KD*), 3rd, critical ed., ed. Heinrich Scholz (1910; reprint, Darmstadt: Wissenschaftliche Buchgesellschaft, 1961), §§ 71–93, 186, 212.

17 *Der christliche Glaube, nach den Grundsätzen der evangelischen Kirche im Zusammenhange dargestellt* (hereafter *CG*, cited by section), 7th ed., based on the 2nd (1830–31), 2 vols. (ed. Martin Redeker; Berlin: Walter de Gruyter, 1960), § 24. Eng. trans. of the 2nd German ed.: *The Christian Faith* (ed. H. R. Mackintosh and J. S. Stewart; Edinburgh: T. & T. Clark, 1928).

18 The ecclesiological contrast appears in *CG,* § 24. For the contrast between word and symbolic action in worship, see *Die christliche Sitte, nach den Grundsätzen der evangelischen Kirche im Zusammenhange dargestellt* (1884), *SW,* 1,12:212;

cf. *Geschichte der Kirche, SW*, 1,11:45–46.

19 "Über den eigenthümlichen Wert und das bindende Ansehen symbolischer Bücher" (1819), in Schleiermacher, *Kleine Schriften und Predigten* (hereafter *KS*), 3 vols. (ed. Hayo Gerdes and Emanuel Hirsch; Berlin: Walter de Gruyter, 1969–70), 2:143–44, 159–62. Nevertheless, against any temptation to exaggerate the perfection of the old confessions, Schleiermacher points out that their authors were men and theologians like us ("An die Herren D.D.D. von Cölln und D. Schulz: Ein Sendschreiben" [1831], *KS*, 2:237–38).

20 *CG*, § 24, Zusatz.

21 *Zugabe zu meinem Schreiben an Herrn Ammon* (1818), *SW*, 1,5:409–10.

22 *An Ammon, SW*, 1,5:345; *Geschichte der Kirche, SW*, 1,11:602.

23 *Geschichte der Kirche, SW*, 1,11:615–16; cf. *CG*, §§ 17, 27–28.

24 See in particular "Theology Within the Limits of Piety Alone: Schleiermacher and Calvin's Notion of God" (1981), *The Old Protestantism,* chap. 12, and "Nature and the Theater of Redemption: Schleiermacher on Christian Dogmatics and the Creation Story" (1987), *Continuing the Reformation,* chap. 9.

25 Sixteen is the number given in the index to the English translation (see n. 17 above). Redeker's index lists fifteen, but that is because he takes as one reference the two citations from Calvin in *CG*, § 119.3. (Neither index includes the third mention of Calvin, without quotation, in this same section.) In Redeker's first reference, § 37 is apparently a slip for § 38. There are also slips – no doubt errors of transcription – in Schleiermacher's own citations from the *Institutes*: in the footnote reference to Calvin in *CG*, § 108.4, the Roman numeral IX should of course be IV; the second Calvin quotation in § 119.3 is from the *Institutes,* book three, chapter 21 (not chap. 23); the quotation at the head of § 141 is from book four, chapter 17 (not chap. 7).

26 *CG*, § 43.1.

27 *Inst.*, 1.14.6–11.

28 *CG*, § 43.2.

29 *CG*, § 45.2 (with reference to *Inst.*, 1.14.17–18).

30 *CG*, § 140.4. At the beginning of the following section (§ 141), Schleiermacher quotes Calvin – among others – on the effects of the Lord's Supper, but without subsequent comment.

31 *CG*, §§ 40.2, 55.1 n., 72.4 n., 81.1 n., 108.4, 109.4 n. Calvin is also cited (with implicit approval) for his assertion that belief in providence, no less than creation, distinguishes Christians from unbelievers (§ 38).

32 "Über die Lehre von der Erwählung," etc., reproduced in *SW*, 1,2:393–484. It is in this article that Schleiermacher mentions the description of him as a 'bold and resolute disciple of Calvin,' adding, 'I do not know with what justice' (p. 399).

33 *CG*, §§ 117–18. For the notion of a *verschwindender Gegensatz*, see § 118.1.

34 *CG*, § 119.2. Schleiermacher recognizes that the qualification he introduces

resembles the view Calvin rejects as childish: that the idea of election is unobjectionable if no one is actually condemned (*Inst.*, 3.23.1).

35 *CG*, § 119.3.

36 Ibid. (The expression *eine völlig atomistische Ansicht des Erlösungswerkes* appears later, in § 120.2.) Schleiermacher finds Calvin's 'formula' logical enough, and he clearly sympathizes with his refusal to accept the attempts commonly made to soften the doctrine of predestination. If the operations of divine grace end at death, then the logical conclusion can only be that some are predestined to damnation, others to blessedness; and it does not help to argue that the former are passed over, not foreordained to damnation, or that God merely 'foreknows' their fate. For Schleiermacher, however, the doctrine is made tolerable – i.e., consistent with the Christian consciousness – by denying the premise that death ends the work of grace. Hence § 119 concludes with a pointer to the eschatological doctrines he will take up later (see in particular the appendix to § 163).

37 Concerning the relation of Edwards himself to the theological legacy of Calvin, we have his own direct testimony in the preface to his *Freedom of the Will* (1754). He accepts the party label 'Calvinist' (in distinction from 'Arminian') but disclaims dependence on Calvin: he neither holds his doctrines merely because Calvin taught them nor believes everything exactly as Calvin taught.

38 See, for instance, his remarks in Charles Hodge, *Systematic Theology* (hereafter *ST*), 3 vols. (1871–72; reprint, Grand Rapids, Mich.: Wm. B. Eerdmans, 1981), 2:440–41. I have explored Hodge's relation to Schleiermacher more fully in a paper, "Charles Hodge and the Europeans," presented at the Hodge symposium held in Princeton, 22–24 October 1997, published in John W. Stewart and James H. Moorehead, eds., *Charles Hodge Revisited: A Critical Appraisal of His Life and Work* (Grand Rapids, Mich.: Wm. B. Eerdmans, 2002).

39 Hodge explains that the old Latin divines had the characteristic merits of 'the American, or what is the same thing, the British mind', Hodge, "Neander's History," *Biblical Repertory and Princeton Review* 16 (1844): 155–83; quotations on pp. 182–83.

40 *CC*, §§ 21, 25 (*Zusatz*), 27; cf. *KD*, §§ 60, 203–8.

41 See, for instance, *ST*, 2:479. To preserve his claim that he presents simply what 'has always been the faith of the Church,' Hodge is sometimes obliged to unchurch not only the rationalists (as here), but even Roman Catholics, Lutherans, and (implicitly) the Eastern Orthodox (2:367, 373, 418, 450–51, 621).

42 *ST*, 1:394–97.

43 *ST*, 3:131–34 (on justification).

44 In the long section on the Lord's Supper (*ST*, vol. 3, part 3, chap. 20, §§ 15–19), the index omits some of the pages on which Calvin is named (pp. 639, 645, 656, 676 n.3), or named and quoted (pp. 641, 646). There may well be other omissions that I have not noticed.

45 *ST*, 3:373; 3:90, 369 n.1, 389, 596; 3:487, 501, 580; 2:209; 3:629–30; 1:467, 3:631.

46 *ST*, 2:209.

47 *ST*, 3:3–5.

48 *ST*, 3:630.

49 *ST*, 3:371.

50 *ST*, 3:596.

51 *Inst.*, 4.16.17–26. By the end of this segment of book 4, chapter 16, Calvin can speak confidently of 'the dogma we have now established concerning the regeneration of infants'. Though Hodge does not cite Calvin's teaching on infant baptism, as he does Calvin's teaching on the Lord's Supper, the conclusion to his preceding section, on baptism as a means of grace (*ST*, 3:590), is in close agreement with Calvin.

52 *ST*, 3:646–47.

53 The pertinent documents, including the Articles of the *Consensus* and Calvin's exposition of them (i.e., his *Defensio sanae et orthodoxae doctrinae de sacramentis, etc.,* 1555), will be found in *OS*, 2:24, 1–87. On Calvin's intention in writing the *Expositio*, see p. 267.

54 B. A. Gerrish, *Tradition and the Modern World: Reformed Theology in the Nineteenth Century* (Chicago: University of Chicago Press, 1978), 57–65.

55 Charles Hodge, "Doctrine of the Reformed Church on the Lord's Supper," *Biblical Repertory 20* (1848): 227–78; quotations from p. 251. Hodge also dismissed the distinction, crucial to Calvin's doctrine, between 'believing' and 'eating' as a 'distinction without a difference' (*ST*, 3:644–45).

56 John W. Nevin, *The Mystical Presence: A Vindication of the Reformed or Calvinistic Doctrine of the Holy Eucharist* (Philadelphia: J. B. Lippincott, 1846), 155–63. Nevin traced the difficulties under which Calvin's theory laboured to a 'false psychology,' and he believed that his proposed revisions rested on a scientific psychology.

57 Nevin, "Doctrine of the Reformed Church on the Lord's Supper," *Mercersburg Review* 2 (1850): 421–548, p. 523.

58 James Hastings Nichols, *Romanticism in American Theology: Nevin and Schaff at Mercersburg* (Chicago: University of Chicago Press, 1961), 89–91.

59 Hodge, "Doctrine of the Reformed Church," 273. It must be added, however, that if Nevin overestimated the significance of Calvin's doctrine of the Lord's Supper in this respect, Hodge's refutation of Nevin underestimates Calvin's doctrine of the preached word (see Gerrish, *Tradition and the Modern World*, 62–63). In his *Mystical Presence* (p. 75) Nevin cited Schleiermacher in his support, who understood the Calvinistic Supper to affirm *die nirgend sonst zu habende wirkliche Gegenwart seines Leibes und Blutes* (*CG*, § 140.4).

60 See J[ohn] F. Jensen, *Calvin's Doctrine of the Work of Christ* (London: James

Clarke, 1956), especially pp. 51–58. For a different estimate of the role of the *munus triplex* in the 1559 *Institutes,* see Klauspeter Blaser, *Calvins Lehre von den drei Ämtern Christi,* Theologische Studien, no. 105 (Zurich: EVZ–Verlag, 1970).

61 *ST,* 2:461.

62 See *CG,* §§ 100–2, especially § 102.3.

63 *Responsio ad Balduini convicia* (1562), *CO,* 9:576. The one child of Calvin's marriage to Idelette de Bure lived only a few days.

64 In *ST,* 2:166, Hodge mentions without comment the 'celebrated formula' of the semi-Pelagian Vincent of Lérins (d. ca. 450): 'Quod ubique, quod semper, quod ab omnibus creditum est.' Though he does not here endorse the formula, he comes close to it in his characteristic appeal to what the Church has always taught (see n. 41 above).

65 *CG,* § 131.2. Schleiermacher understood the development (*Entwicklung*) of doctrine not simply as an observable historical phenomenon, but as a theological task (see, e.g., *KD,* §§ 177–82), which, by definition, both holds the theologian responsible to authorized ecclesiastical doctrines and frees him from being *nur em Träger der Überlieferung* (*ibid.,* § 19). In *KD,* § 29, he speaks of 'mindless tradition' (*geistlose Überlieferung*). But the implicit contrast between *Überlieferung* and *Entwicklung* does not mean that 'tradition' always carried negative connotations for Schleiermacher (see for instance *CG,* § 127.2, *KD,* § 47). See also the references on orthodoxy and heterodoxy in n. 40 above.

66 See, e.g., Calvin to Martin Seidemann, 14 March 1555, *CO,* 15:501–2.

67 Calvin to Francis Burkhardt, 27 February 1555, *CO,* 15:454.

68 *Defensio sanae et orthodoxae doctrinae de servitute et liberatione humani arbitrii adversus calumnia Alberti Pighii Campensis* (1543), *CO,* 6:250. See further my article, "The Pathfinder: Calvin's Image of Martin Luther" (1968), reprinted in *The Old Protestantism,* chap. 2.

69 Continuity may, of course, be located in the questions asked rather than in the answers given, and of this the doctrine of election is a prime example. Preoccupation with the divine decrees and efficacious grace has been characteristic of Reformed theology from Calvin to Barth, but it has largely taken the form of a continuing attempt to *revise* Calvin's doctrine. Elsewhere, I have suggested that continuity in Reformed theology might also be sought less in the preservation of a short list of distinctive doctrines, more in the 'habit of mind' brought to the doctrinal task. See B. A. Gerrish, "Tradition in the Modern World: The Reformed Habit of Mind," in *Toward the Future of Reformed Theology: Tasks, Topics, Traditions,* (ed. David Willis and Michael Welker; Grand Rapids, Mich.: Wm. B. Eerdmans, 1999), 3–20.

70 I am grateful to Philip Butin for his spirited response to the first version of this essay, presented at the Calvin Studies Society Colloquium on 24 April 1999. The

response and the subsequent discussion showed that he and I start out with some differences. Perhaps they could be resolved, but I cannot take them up here. The few changes I have made only attempt to make clearer what I was arguing in the paper – and what I was not arguing.

3

RADICAL REFORMED ORTHODOXY[1]

Duncan B. Forrester

There is in Scotland a theological tradition which at its beginning was probably the most radical strain in the mainstream Calvinist movement. In certain ways it was markedly too radical for Calvin himself![2] Down the centuries this radical theological tradition has been tamed in a variety of ways, but again and again there have been at least partial retrievals of the Scots tradition of interlocking theological, ecclesiastical, social and political radicalism combined with a strong confessional orthodoxy. One of these partial revivals may be taking place today, with the coming of devolution and all the hope and excitement this has engendered. In this paper I want to examine Scottish radical orthodoxy by way of some forays into history, and ask how far it is alive today, or can be retrieved. Is the distinctive 'radical orthodoxy' of Scottish Calvinism relevant and recoverable in the circumstances of the early twenty-first century?

A recent, high profile and very lively, largely Anglo-Catholic theological movement led by John Milbank which labels itself 'Radical Orthodoxy' has emerged and is sending shock waves of excitement throughout the Anglo-American theological scene. The orthodoxy that they affirm is 'credal orthodoxy,' apparently very much that of the high Middle Ages. On this basis, they have the ambitious project of 'recovering and extending a fully Christianised ontology and practical philosophy consonant with authentic Christian doctrine.'[3] The radicalism they espouse involves going back to the roots, particularly the patristic and early medieval roots, of the theological tradition, 'and especially to the Augustinian vision of all knowledge as divine illumination', thus hoping to overcome destructive modern dualisms.[4] They claim to be radical also in that they believe that the tradition needs to be rethought, because its 'collapse' at the end of the Middle Ages betrayed serious weaknesses which must now be remedied. They are in revolt against 'the self-conscious superficiality of today's secularism'. Indeed they stand in conscious opposition to the modern world and the modernist or liberal theology which they believe makes fatal compromises with modernity, almost after the style of the First Vatican Council. What I do *not* see in this movement of 'radical orthodoxy' is a serious social, political and economic radicalism understood as direct implications of an orthodox theology.

That was the kind of radical orthodoxy which was at the heart of the Scottish Reformation, and also had deep pre-Reformation roots in the Scottish tradition. At the time of the Reformation, it was generally assumed among Calvinists that the confession of the Lordship of Christ demanded through-going reform of church, society, and state, as well as personal conversion of the individual. Christian orthodoxy was seen as inherently radical, neither a pietist retreat into individualism nor a liberal compromise with the powers, but a serious project to reshape church, society and the individual in accordance with Christian truth. The Scots Reformers set out to change the world as well as the Church in the light of the gospel. And that is exactly what they did.

This paper is an essay in contextual theology, attempting to trace in broad outline the changing contours of the radical theological tradition in Scotland. But it also addresses the question whether this tradition in modified form can be retrieved not just in Scotland, but more widely as an important resource for 'doing the truth' in today's world, with its very different challenges and opportunities from those of the past. The question with which I end will also be seen, I hope, as a challenge.

The Scots Reformation

To a far greater extent than in England or in most continental European countries, the Scottish Reformation was a popular movement, a Reformation from below rather than a religious change imposed from above by the Crown on a puzzled and sometimes resistant populace. The Scots Reformers were able to ride a mood of extreme disenchantment with the old church and a profound questioning of the social, political and economic orders, so vividly portrayed in Sir David Lindsay's drama *Ane Satyre of the Thrie Estaites* [1540], wonderfully revived at the first Edinburgh Festival.[5] At the turning point of this drama, John the Commonweal, the ordinary poor Scot, supported by Gude Counsel and Divine Correctioun, grasping the book of the gospels, denounces in turn the oppression and exploitation of the nobles, the burgesses, and the church, and calls for a purification of church and state which will be both a reformation of the church and the establishment of justice for the poor and the weak in Scottish society.[6] At the end, poor John is vindicated as representative of all the poor and forgotten in Scotland:

> Give John the Common-Weal ane gay garmoun,
> Because the Common-Weal has been owrelookit,
> That is the cause that Common-Weal is cruikit.
> With singular profit he has been sae suppressit,
> That he is baith cauld, nakit and disgysit.[7]

The Reformation which was already beginning when *The Thrie Estaites* was first performed in 1540, quickly developed into a populist movement which the Reformers did not find hard to harness to their purposes, and make into a 'reformation from below.'[8] This movement was as much about justice for the poor and liberation for the oppressed as it was about the reform of the church and its doctrine; radical Reformed orthodoxy was regarded as a total package, in Peter Matheson's words, 'less a shopping-list of demands than the choreography for a new dance'.[9] Humanists such as George Buchanan were attracted to Calvinism because it seemed to offer the possibility of realising their utopian hopes, and blended easily with their humanism. There was also the fact that the Scots Reformers drew heavily on a particular strand of late medieval conciliar and nominalist thought, particularly as mediated by the influential Scots theologian, John Mair, who taught mainly in the University of Paris and is believed to have taught both Calvin and Ignatius Loyola. There was thus an earlier Scottish radical and democratic tradition which easily fed into 'Reformed Radical Orthodoxy.'

The monarch, remaining thirled to the old faith, was at odds with a multitude of her people, led by a section of the middle nobility and Reformers who were on the radical wing of the Genevan Reformation. The Crown in Scotland fairly consistently opposed the Reformation, but was never capable of effective resistance or of restoring Catholicism, as happened in England under Mary Tudor.

In this context it was not, perhaps, surprising that the Scots Reformation actually affirmed a *duty* of resistance to tyranny. In the Scots Confession we find among the 'Warkis reputit gude befoir God' the saving of innocent lives, the defence of the oppressed, and 'to represse tyrannie', while obedience to superiors is only enjoined when it is not repugnant to God's commands and when the authorities do not 'passe over the bounds of their office',[10] and are 'doing that thing quhilk appertains to [their] charge'.[11]

This is developed by Knox into a positive duty of resistance to tyrants and unjust rulers. Calvin himself had made a cautious concession in affirming that in closely circumscribed cases the elected magistrates might legitimately resist a tyrant;[12] this was now extended immeasurably by Knox in affirming that the people at large have a duty not only to support magistrates in resisting a tyrant, but they may themselves initiate resistance. On the basis of a covenantal understanding of society, Knox is able to appeal first to the nobility and then to the populace of Scotland in general to resist the despotic rule of Mary Stuart.[13] Resistance to tyranny and oppression was an obligation, for failure to oppose unrighteousness in the covenanted community involved complicity in injustice and placed the citizenry along with their rulers under the judgement of God. A sacred duty is laid on each citizen who is part of the covenanted community to take part in resisting and removing idolatrous and tyrannical authorities. And as in many places in the Bible, idolatry is closely linked to oppression and the doing of injustice.

This idea that the civil community was bound to God in a covenantal relationship implied, of course, that the whole life of the community was to be shaped by God's commands and should reflect the divine purpose of justice and of love. Thus the second foundational document of the Scottish Reformation alongside the Scots Confession was the First Book of Discipline of 1560.[14] This was a blueprint for church and society in Scotland, outlining the organisation of the new Reformed church, and how it would exercise what the Scots Confession saw as a third mark of the True Church, 'Ecclesiastical discipline uprightlie ministred', from which no one in Scotland was to be exempt.[15] And it was so at the beginning: ecclesiastical discipline was exercised in cases of cheating merchants or oppressive landlords as well as in cases of fornication, adultery, and sabbath-breaking. Among the offences that The First Book of Discipline regarded as the concerns of church courts were 'oppressing of the poore by exactions', and 'deceiving of them in buying and selling by wrang met and measure'.[16] In the terms of the day, there was here a preferential option for the poor. Everyone in the realm, rulers and preachers as well as the poor, were to be subject to discipline. Through discipline, broadly understood, society with its social, political and economic structures was to be reformed.[17]

Knox was not afraid to emphasise human equality in the most emphatic terms. The poor have as much responsibility before God as the powerful for the spiritual and moral state of the nation as they have equal worth in the eyes of God.[18] The nation as a whole in solidarity is responsible to God:

> And if ye think that ye are innocent because ye are not the chief authors of such iniquity, ye are utterly deceived. For God doth not only punish the chief offenders, but with them doth He damn the consenters to iniquity; and all are judged to consent that knowing impiety committed give no testimony that the same displeaseth them. To speak this matter more plain, as your princes and rulers are criminal with your bishops of all idolatry committed, and of all the innocent blood that is shed for the testimony of Christ's truth, and that because they maintain them in their tyranny, so are you (I mean so many of you as give no plain confession to the contrary) criminal and guilty with your princes and rulers of the same crimes, because ye assist and maintain your princes in their blind rage and give no declaration that their tyranny displeaseth you.[19]

It is not inappropriate to see in these emphases on human equality and the collective responsibility of the community roots of modern democratic politics.

For both theological and prudential reasons, the Scots reformers rejected from the beginning the idea of royal supremacy over the church. They appealed to and mobilized the nobility and the common people to carry forward the work of reformation in church and society. Yet they were also eager for a 'godly prince', and in James VI & I they believed for a time they had found such a one. But although the godly prince had, they affirmed, clear duties to assist and support godliness and true religion, the prince could not possess spiritual authority within the church and should not be regarded, after the fashion of many Lutheran principalities on the continent, as *primus episcopus*. Nor was the prince to be seen as supreme as much in ecclesiastical matters as in temporal affairs, as in England.

Once again the Scottish Reformation is shown to be more intrinsically radical than the English Reformation that finds its theological rationale in Richard Hooker's *Laws of Ecclesiastical Polity*. Nor is it similar to the situation in Lutheran polities, which recognise a sharp distinction between the two kingdoms. It is determined to preserve the prophetic freedom of the church. It even radically revises Calvin's own account of the two kingdoms and their relation:

> ... let us observe that in man government is two-fold: the one spiritual, by
> which the conscience is trained to piety and divine worship; the other civil,
> by which the individual is instructed in those duties which, as men and
> citizens, we are bound to perform. ... To these two forms are commonly
> given the not inappropriate names of spiritual and temporal jurisdiction,
> intimating that the former species has reference to the life of the soul, while
> the latter relates to matters of the present life, not only to food and clothing,
> but to the enacting of laws which require a man to live among his fellows
> purely, honourably, and modestly. The former has its seat within the soul, the
> latter only regulates the external conduct. We may call the one the spiritual,
> the other the civil kingdom.[20]

Thus for Calvin both kingdoms are expressions of God's care and love for
human beings, and in a sense they are complementary. Calvin agrees with
Luther (if rather less emphatically!) that the two kingdoms must not be
confused. They 'are always to be viewed apart from each other. When the
one is considered, we should call off our minds, and not allow them to think
of the other.'[21]

But in Scotland a rather different account of the relation between the
two kingdoms was there from the time of the Reformation. Theology and
the gospel are not the concerns of the spiritual realm alone; they are the
basis for a *confessional* politics and a *confessional* economics, based on
an unashamedly christological foundation. The Scots Confession is thus in
interesting ways comparable to The Theological Declaration of Barmen of
1934. Perhaps this is what attracted Barth to it in 1937.

The working out in Scotland of the theory of two kingdoms in terms of
church-state relations is also distinctive and radical. The basic position is that
the power of the crown may be, and sometimes must be, confronted, even
while honouring and respecting the office. Andrew Melville, the leader of
the Second Reformation, who in an encounter with James VI at Falkland in
1596 called the king 'bot God's sillie vassall', typified the early relationship
between church and state. Melville sees his task at a time of crisis for church
and crown to speak truth to power and clarify what he sees as the true
Reformed relationship of church and state. He addresses the king:

And, thairfor, Sir, as divers tymes befor, sa now again, I mon tell yow, thair is twa Kings and twa Kingdomes in Scotland. Thair is Chryst Jesus the King, and his kingdome the Kirk, whase subject King James the Saxt is, and of whase kingdome nocht a king, nor a lord, nor a heid, bot a member! And they whome Chryst hes callit and commandit to watch over his Kirk, and governe his spirituall kingdome, hes sufficient powar of him, and authoritie sa to do, bathe togidder and severalie; the quhilk na Christian King nor Prince sould controll and discharge, but fortifie and assist, utherwayes nocht fathfull subjects nor members of Christ.[22]

Here is a strong affirmation of the sole Lordship of Christ, and a powerful suggestion that this is mediated to the civil authorities by the Kirk, which in a special sense is the Kingdom of Christ. This distinctively Scottish version of the two kingdoms theory may from time to time have been open to the opposite dangers to those latent in the Anglican Reformation's affirmation of the royal supremacy.[23] It certainly involved a claim on the part of the church to spiritual independence, which was seen by royalists in the sixteenth and seventeenth centuries as an unacceptable limitation on royal power. Because in the seventeenth century they were used as agents of royal control, bishops were – and are often still – seen in the Presbyterian mind as infringing both the freedom of the church and its populist, democratic polity as a folk-church. As a consequence, Scotland had four and a half centuries of controversy about the authority of the Crown, of parliament, and of the civil courts over the Church of Scotland.

Thus the sixteenth century Reformation period established a sharp distinction between the spheres of church and state, yet spoke of the mutual responsibilities that they had for each other. Scotland was to be a Christian commonwealth in which the activities of church and state were to be complementary. The church was to be responsible for education at all levels, for the relief of poverty, and for the maintenance of moral standards, as well as for the worship of God and the preaching of sound doctrine. The state had the responsibility for defence, for most serious matters of law and order, and for legislation in temporal matters. Much depended on smooth co-operation between church and state in their separate roles.

All this depended on a particularly strong christological emphasis in the early Scottish Reformation documents. The universal lordship of Christ, or 'the crown rights of the Redeemer', are constantly affirmed. At the heart of the 'Action Prayer' in the Book of Common Order of 1564, commonly called 'Knox's Liturgy', worshippers come to his table to declare and witness before the world that by him alone we have received liberty and life; that by him alone thou dost acknowledge us as thy children and heirs; that by him alone we have entrance to the throne of thy grace; that by him alone we are possessed in our spiritual kingdom to eat and drink at his table, with whom we have our conversation presently in heaven, and by whom our bodies shall be raised up again from the dust, and shall be placed with him in that endless joy which thou, O Father of mercy, hast prepared for thine elect before the foundation of the world was laid.[24]

A National Covenant

If the sixteenth-century Reformation Settlement suggested that the Church of Scotland was more a folk-church than a state church, the seventeenth century through the development of ideas of covenant, expressed especially in the National Covenant of 1638 and the Solemn League and Covenant of 1643, saw Scotland as a nation under God, bound together in faithfulness to God's covenant, with a national church at the heart of its life. The two covenants were understood also as a protest by the nation particularly against policies which limited the freedom of the church. The Revolution of 1688 recognised and affirmed the Church of Scotland's understanding of itself as a national church and a folk-church which had a sphere distinct from that of the state within which it was and must be free. Church and state had responsibilities towards one another, responsibilities that could only be exercised if there was separation.

The radical populist and democratic emphasis continues close to the heart of seventeenth-century Scottish theology and political theory. The christocentric biblical theology of the earliest Reformation documents such as the Scots Confession is now replaced with a more scholastic Calvinism, and the new form of federal Calvinism expressed in the Westminster documents of the 1640s is on the face of it apparently less radical. But Samuel Rutherford, the pre-eminent covenanting theologian of the seventeenth century, is unambiguously radical in social and political matters and combines this with an emotional and passionate Calvinist piety, particularly as expressed in his immensely influential *Letters*. His *Lex Rex* (1644) was one of the most significant seventeenth-century works on political theology, which aroused intense antagonism particularly after the Restoration because it was interpreted as an anti-royalist diatribe. In fact *Lex Rex* developed systematically and in relation to radically changed circumstances the theological and political radicalism we already found in Knox. The underlying theology was, however, significantly different. In almost medieval style it was assumed that there was a large overlap between Scripture and natural law. 'The Scripture's arguments,' he wrote, 'may be drawn out of the school of nature'.[25] No trace here of Barth's rejection three centuries after of natural law and natural theology! But on this basis, Rutherford affirms popular sovereignty. Kings do not rule by divine right, but have delegated power mediated from God through the people. Although he teaches that the people have 'irrevocably made over to the king' the powers of government, it still remains true that in the exercise of executive power the king is highly circumscribed. Indeed in Rutherford we find a quite clear form of the separation of powers, a constitutional theory which has more clearly Calvinist roots than is sometimes acknowledged.[26]

Rutherford develops systematically, and in dialogue with continental thinkers, particularly Calvinists and Jesuits, what had been more cautiously suggested in the early Scottish Reformation documents – that there is a positive duty to resist an unjust and oppressive tyrant. This duty is normally (as Calvin himself suggested) laid on the subordinate magistrates and the estates; only in really extreme situations may a private citizen resist the established authorities. The argument, as Coffey points out, is based on natural law and on Roman law almost as much as upon Scripture, and Rutherford is at pains to combat suggestions that passages of the Bible like Romans 13 are in fact admonitions to passive obedience.[27]

Rutherford also develops the radical Scottish tradition through what Coffey calls his 'genuine passion for social justice'.[28] The central role of the monarch and the judges is to do justice, particularly to the poor. In order to do this they must live near the poor and appreciate their condition. The oppression of the poor and weak is closely linked, as in the sixteenth-century Scots Reformation documents (and indeed in the Old Testament), to idolatry, which it is the duty of those in authority to extirpate.

Establishment and Disruption

With the establishment of Presbyterianism in Scotland as part of the Revolution Settlement of 1690, the Church of Scotland became a very central part of the power structures of the nation. The General Assembly assumed a role which it is only now relinquishing – that of a quasi-parliament, articulating the voice of the Scottish people on a variety of issues, not exclusively theological and ecclesiastical. A radical prophetic voice was heard less frequently and the political authorities and the landowners successfully established control over the appointment of many ministers. The literati of the Scottish Enlightenment such as Adam Smith sang the praises of the Presbyterian polity and the virtues of the Presbyterian clergy. These they saw as foundational to a lively, intellectual and open society. But clearly they did not expect the Kirk or its ministers to provide radical prophetic criticism of the social and political order. In *The Wealth of Nations* (1776) Adam Smith declared that 'There is scarce perhaps to be found anywhere in Europe a more learned, decent, independent, and respectable set of men than the greater part of the Presbyterian clergy of Holland, Geneva, Switzerland and Scotland.'[29] These are not wild radicals, Knoxes or Rutherfords. Rather, they commend themselves to their 'superiors' by 'their learning, the irreproachable regularity of their life, and by the faithful and diligent discharge of their duty.' The ministers 'have more influence over the minds of the common people than perhaps the clergy of any other established church.' For 'the common people look upon him with that kindness with which we naturally regard one who approaches somewhat to our own condition, but who, we think, ought to be in a higher.'[30] The radical prophets of the Reformation and covenanting times had become pillars of the community!

The Scottish Enlightenment did not, however, uniformly oppose the Scots radical tradition. Influential teachers and savants like Frances Hutcheson and Millar presented a theologically-informed philosophy which was full of radical implications. Their disciples often enough maintained the radical tradition, particularly outside Scotland, in America for instance where several of them were stirrers up of revolutionary fervour. At home, in Scotland most energies went into church-state disputes, rather than social reform.[31] Ecclesiastically there was more tension in the church about the people's right to call their minister than Adam Smith recognised. The Secessions of the eighteenth century were not only about the people's right to call their ministers but about the democratic structure of the church, about human equality and about the need to preserve independence from the state and indeed the landed gentry.

The populist, radical tradition thus survived, if with some difficulty, in the eighteenth century. One may argue that this was less true of Scotland than among the radical Irish Presbyterians who, inspired by the French

Revolution, supported the 1798 Uprising, or in the American Revolution under the influence of John Witherspoon and others.

Theologically, a modified scholastic Calvinism was almost the foundational premise of the Scottish Enlightenment, which in its main thrust was certainly not hostile to the church or to Christian faith.[32] But the philosophy and the theology of the Scottish Enlightenment preserved little of the radical impulse of the sixteenth and seventeenth centuries.

Among the faithful the radical tradition survived here and there. It began to come alive in the Highlands when landlords, usually strongly supported by the ministers they had appointed to 'their' parishes, began to clear the people from their estates to make way for sheep and other 'improvements.' The widespread sense of outrage at what was happening led to a considerable proportion of the people of the Highlands joining the Free Church when the Church of Scotland split in 1843 on the issue of relations to the state. In the Free Church there was a cautious revival of the radical tradition, the belief that Calvinist orthodoxy has prophetic things to say in relation to the social order and the broader community.

It was, as I say, a *cautious* revival. Thomas Chalmers and the other leaders were almost obsessed with the dangers of public disorder arising from ecclesiastical disputes, and Chalmers' life-long defence of Establishment was an assertion that the established church should provide through the parish system the sinews of the social order, which in a way was a continuation of the tradition of The First Book of Discipline.

Chalmers' own social thought was conservative; he saw the social as well as the economic system as part of the divine ordering of things, and thus as beyond theological question.[33] At the laying of the foundation stone of New College, Edinburgh, he declared:

> We leave to others the passions and politics of this world, and nothing will ever be taught, I trust, in any of our [theological] halls, which shall have the remotest tendency to disturb the existing order of things, or to confound the ranks and distinctions which now obtain in society.[34]

Chalmers was as significant in his day in political economy as in theology; he was one of the leaders in what Boyd Hilton calls 'the baptism of political economy',[35] and he even received the accolade of being denounced by Marx as 'the arch-Parson Thomas Chalmers', a pupil of 'Parson Malthus'.[36]

Chalmers taught political economy as a branch of natural theology, just as Adam Smith taught natural theology as part of moral philosophy.[37] For Chalmers, natural theology was so closely associated with classical political economy as to be almost indistinguishable from it. The clear implication of this was, of course, that the market (and perhaps behind that, the social order as a whole) was a kind of divine ordering, and therefore to that extent beyond human critique or control. 'The whole science of Political Economy', he wrote, 'is full of those exquisite adaptations to the wants and the comforts of human life, which bespeak the skill of a master-hand, in the adjustment of its laws, and the working of its profoundly constructed mechanism.'[38] The workings of the market point to a beneficent God who gives good gifts to his children through market transactions, which harness human self-interest to the achievement of the common good. Thus the selfishness of human beings results in 'cheapening and multiplying to the uttermost all the articles of human enjoyment, and establishing a thousand reciprocities of mutual interest in the world'; accordingly it displays 'the benevolence and comprehensive wisdom of God.'[39] The market, as part of the providential ordering of a just and loving God, is beyond critique, and should be left undisturbed to pursue its benign course.

In addition to this sacralising of economic processes, Chalmers was also one of the leading figures in commending a way to combat what people at the time called 'pauperism.' The term is significant. It suggests that the problem is *poor people*, who develop in an industrial society communities and cultures and patterns of behaviour which actually perpetuate and exacerbate poverty. Essentially, Chalmers taught, pauperism is caused, not by society or economic structures, or by injustice but by interference with economic processes. By 'trying to mend the better mechanism which nature had instituted', evils such as the multiplication of pauperism are engendered.[40] The Poor Law taking the place of private and ecclesiastical charity, Chalmers believed, simply makes the situation worse, as do common patterns of behaviour and attitudes among poor people themselves. The solution to pauperism is also largely in the hands of the poor themselves; charity and government intervention often do more harm than good. Official policies of relief, which usually ran counter to 'economic laws,' make the situation worse. In Malthusian tones, Chalmers declared:

There is no possible help for them [the poor] if they will not help themselves. It is to a rise and reformation in the habits of our peasantry that we look for deliverance, and not to the impotent crudities of a speculative legislation ... This will at length save the country from the miseries of a redundant population – and this we apprehend, to be the great, the only specific for its worst moral and its worst political disorders.[41]

'The remedy against the extension of pauperism', he declares elsewhere,

does not lie in the liberalities of the rich; it lies in the hearts and habits of the poor. Plant in their bosoms a principle of independence. Give a high tone of delicacy to their characters. Teach them to recoil from pauperism as a degradation.[42]

The state and the broader community are not responsible for 'pauperism,' nor is its solution in their hands: 'Neither government nor the higher classes of the state, have any share in those economical distresses to which every trading and manufacturing nation is exposed', for 'the high road to the secure and permanent prosperity of labourers, is through the medium of their own sobriety, and intelligence, and virtue.'[43]

Paupers have no claim in justice; only on the compassion of their neighbours, most desirably expressed in Chalmers' view through a revitalised parish system. The local community, best represented by the parishes of an established church in which the rich and the poor are held together in mutual responsibility, was the most appropriate agency for *disciplining* and caring for paupers, for the local community knew the individuals and families concerned, as well as local conditions, and could adapt their treatment appropriately. The church, in Chalmers' thought, while it had close relations to the state, was in essentials a body independent of the state. In spiritual and moral matters it had its own proper sphere, in which the state should not interfere.

Pauperism and economic distress were caused by well-intentioned tinkerings with God-given systems, and the solution depended upon the character of the poor and a true, that is Christian, account of human nature, together with the moral paternalism of an established church which was concerned with nurturing the poor in virtue and responding wisely and guardedly to the misery of the poorest.

We have in Chalmers an example of a kind of theology, which was immensely influential in its day. It rested on an apparently Calvinist/ Augustinian account of human nature, but it embraced and endorsed almost without qualification the dominant contemporary economic and social theories. Its central problem was that which Barth identified a century later: a free-floating natural theology has an in-built tendency to sanctify existing orders and to assimilate to secular theories and philosophies. Chalmers' social theology in fact owed as much to Adam Smith as to the gospel, and it suggested behaviour towards the poor that was often callous and even cynical rather than generous. Perhaps Donald Macleod is right in suggesting that it is not theology at all, because '[Chalmers] is merely lending the weight of his authority as a churchman to a purely secular economic theory'.[44] Certainly Chalmers' social theology has few links with the strong christological emphasis of the early Scottish Reformation. It also had very tenuous links with the populist strand in the radical Calvinist theological tradition in Scotland, except (and this is important) that it continued to put the issue of poverty high on the church's agenda.

And yet the radical tradition continued in the nineteenth century. Chartists marched to their rallies singing metrical psalms, behind banners bearing the symbols of the Covenanters, and their speeches in Scotland were permeated with biblical imagery and symbols.[45] Keir Hardie, the leader of the Independent Labour Party frequently proclaimed that his socialism was founded on Christian insights. John Philip, Scottish congregationalist, campaigned for the rights of 'natives' in South Africa. In America, evangelical Presbyterians were among the leading abolitionists, drawing on the anti-slavery lectures of the Scottish Enlightenment teachers in the ancient Scottish universities.

Two World Wars

My colleague, Stewart J. Brown, has done pioneering research on the Scottish churches in the years after the First World War and the lead-up to the Union of 1929 between the Church of Scotland and the United Free Church.[46] The aftermath of the war and the beginning of the Depression led to widespread disillusion with the Christian faith and the recognition that the economic and social problems facing British society were indeed very deep-seated. On the whole the Scottish churches were reluctant to engage prophetically with such problems, and their main response to the General

Strike of 1926 was to remain 'impartial,' to help with relief, and to conduct evangelistic campaigns. The United Free Church Moderator that year, Dr George Morrison, after delivering an address on 'Revival,' 'held the balance evenly, and ... charmed everyone by the happiness of his remarks' when the Assembly was addressed, first by the Prime Minister, Stanley Baldwin, and then by a delegation from the Union of Scottish Mine Workers.[47] Shortly afterwards, while the strike was still on, the Moderator took part in an evangelistic campaign in the Fife coalfields, where his lace and ruffles attracted a good deal of ribald attention![48]

Brown suggests that Presbyterian church leaders in the 1920s and early 30s were concerned that their relation with government should not be hampered by any intemperate or one-sided statements, or a prophetic radicalism which might forfeit government support for the projected union. More ominously perhaps, the reunited Church of Scotland declared itself to be 'a national Church representative of the Christian Faith of the Scottish people'.[49] This often went along with strong feeling against Irish Roman Catholics as an alien importation into a racially and religiously unified Scotland. It was even suggested in an article in the Church of Scotland magazine *Life and Work* in 1934 that the Scottish church union of 1929 was the model for the union that the Nazis had forced on the German Protestant churches!

A major turning-point was the Oxford Conference on Church, Community and State of 1937. For some significant Scottish church leaders, this was their first real exposure to ecumenism, and it gave them an opportunity to hear at first hand what anti-Semitism and racism were doing in Germany. Some who had colluded with the anti-Irish and anti-Roman Catholic policies came to their senses. Most from this time came to see Scottish theology and Scottish church life in a broader global frame, and to understand themselves as in some sense accountable to the *oikumene*.

During the Second World War the General Assembly established an influential 'Commission for the Interpretation of God's Will in the Present Crisis' with Principal John Baillie as Convener. This marked in the Church of Scotland a new turn to a more radical stance. Baillie called himself a Christian socialist and was unhappy with the conservatism and caution of the church's contributions to public affairs in recent years. The work of the Commission marked the start of a new-style reformism, closely associated with the kind of liberal evangelical theology with which John Baillie and his brother, Donald, were associated.[50] The Iona Community, founded by

George Macleod in 1937 combined a consistently radical stance on political and economic matters, particularly issues of peace, with a concern for the renewal of worship and an interest in the Celtic tradition. Among its more prominent supporters were most of the prominent liberal evangelical theologians of the time, such as John and Donald Baillie.

The liberal evangelical tradition which was dominant in Scottish theology from the late nineteenth century until the 1960s was in general reformist rather than radical in its social and political orientation. It was aware of its Calvinist roots, but tended to be rather uninterested in the theology which emerged from the Scottish Reformation, and to see itself primarily as a contributor to the emerging ecumenical theology which arose out of the German Church Struggle, the Second World War and the missionary movement, and which looked forward to a day when theology would be a common Christian enterprise rather than a series of separate confessional projects.

The fact that Karl Barth chose to base his 1937–8 Gifford Lectures at Aberdeen on the Scots Confession of 1560, by then almost forgotten in Scotland, came as a great surprise.[51] It had not apparently occurred to many Scots theologians themselves that their Reformation heritage might have something to offer to the crises of the mid-twentieth century. The only modern popular edition of the Scots Confession was published as a result.[52] In the 1950s to 70s liberal evangelicalism seemed to give way steadily to a Scottish Barthian movement led by Professor T. F. Torrance. In terms of its outworking in ecclesiastical, social and political matters, however, this Scottish Barthianism was for the most part cautiously conservative. It is symptomatic that the key point at which T. F. Torrance differed from the master was over infant baptism. In the 1950s T. F. Torrance headed a Church of Scotland Special Commission on Baptism which vigorously defended infant baptism and implied a conservative, Christendom-style ecclesiology in radical conflict with Barth's own assumption that Christendom was over and the West was once again a field of mission in which the baptism of infants no longer made acceptable sense.[53] There was, to be true, a revival of Calvin studies in Scotland around scholars such as R. S. Wallace[54] and T. F. Torrance himself, but the political and social radicalism of early Scottish Calvinism did not figure prominently in this revival of Calvin studies, and Scottish Barthianism was in most respects cautiously conservative.

The aftermath of the Second World War found theology and church life in Scotland buoyant, as elsewhere in the West. The theological colleges were full, churches were packed with worshippers, new churches were being built in the housing estates, where the Sunday schools were full to overflowing, and the Church of Scotland membership reached an all-time high in 1957. Little of the disillusion that followed the First World War was in evidence. There was an almost universal conviction that the war had been necessary to destroy a great evil, and there was a widespread feeling that the churches and some theologians had played a significant role in the destruction of Nazism. In particular the dialectical theologians – Barth, Brunner, Bonhoeffer and others – had identified the evil early and had courageously unveiled and denounced the Beast. There was immense confidence that the relatively new ecumenical biblical theology was a major resource for the renewal of the churches and for their social witness. The new ecumenical biblical theology found support both from liberal evangelicals and from Torrance-style Barthians. But in Scotland as elsewhere it came to an end in the 1960s, partly as the consequence of the onslaught of James Barr and others on the received methodological certainties of biblical theology, partly because of what Robert Jenson has called 'the implosion of its energizing institutions' such as the Student Christian Movement, and partly because of a kind of theological capitulation to the secular.

Possibilities of retrieval

I share John de Gruchy's conviction that 'Reformed theology is best understood as a liberating theology that is catholic in its substance, evangelical in principle, and socially engaged and prophetic in its witness'.[55] This kind of theology should prophetically address the power structures and also expose the elements of alienation and false consciousness within the tradition itself.[56] My brief and sketchy history of Scottish theology suggests that this sort of radical orthodoxy has in the past flourished at times of crisis, political, social and ecclesiastical. Periods when the Church has been under attack and bereft of power and influence appear to be the times when the Church and theology have felt free to be prophetic and to express the radical impulse, repossessing the tradition of the Scottish Reformation.

There is little doubt that the Church of Scotland and its theological tradition are today in a state of crisis. Institutional decline has led in many quarters to a failure of nerve. A massive cultural change of seismic proportions has led in one generation to the legacy of Calvin and of Knox that was for centuries a matter of national pride becoming a major embarrassment to many. In the church and in theology there appears to be something of a failure of nerve.

But there are signs within the Church of a revival of radical Reformed orthodoxy. The contribution of the churches and of theology to the long debate about devolution and the future of Scotland was remarkable, with a range of notable figures playing major roles, most notably, perhaps, Canon Kenyon Wright and successive conveners of the Church of Scotland Church and Nation Committee. William Storrar drafted the 1988 Church and Nation report on the Constitution, which argued impressively that there was a distinct Scottish constitutional tradition which was deeply rooted in the history we have been exploring in this chapter. Storrar also established Common Cause, which drew together a 'rainbow coalition' of Scots intellectuals and public figures in the campaign for devolution. And one could go on. Not only are there already seeds of a renewal of radical Reformed orthodoxy, but some fruits are already appearing!

In Scotland today a radical impulse and a sense of community which have clear roots in the Scottish Reformation continue to flourish and be influential in politics. This was evident at the opening of the Scottish Parliament in July 1999. The proceedings were markedly informal, and started with a wonderful rendering by Sheena Wellington of Burns' great song "A man's a man, for a' that", a strongly egalitarian poem which pokes fun at a hierarchical ordering of society and appears to be a secular expression of Calvinist egalitarianism. This was followed by the singing of the hundredth psalm to the Calvinist Genevan 'plain tune' which had its origins in the Calvinist insistence that the people should play an active part in the music of worship as in the life of civil society.

Could this ecclesiastical and theological crisis and the turning point represented by the establishment of the Scottish Parliament be the moment of opportunity for retrieving and repossessing the Scottish tradition of radical orthodoxy? I think and hope that this may be the case. And if this time of crisis in Scotland is a moment of opportunity for retrieval, as in the past, so now, stimuli and resources from outside have their role to play. Liberation theology has clear affinities with the radical tradition we are discussing, and most of its roots are Roman Catholic. More often than is commonly recognised in Scottish history, Presbyterians and Roman Catholics have been at one in affirming the independence of the church from the state, and seeking to restructure society on a Christian basis. Perhaps retrieval of radical Reformed orthodoxy could also be a moment of ecumenical convergence. Nor is it irrelevant that Barth's retrieval of the radical Calvinist tradition has led a Dutch liberal Calvinist, H. M. Kuitert, to see Barth as the godfather of liberation theology and of modern radical political theology in general.[57]

We can learn much from liberation theology about the issues that a radically orthodox Reformed theology should address, in Scotland or elsewhere. And addressing such an agenda can avoid the danger of a scholastic or a universalising renewal of the tradition. Theology needs help in discerning the signs of the times, although it must not neglect its own distinctive contribution to this process. It must be brave enough to name and confront the idolatries of today. It must attend to the tradition even as it listens to the cry of the poor, the weak and the oppressed, the voice of John the Common-weal. And it must have the courage, as did Knox, to address both the ordinary people of Scotland and the powers.

Notes

1 I am very grateful to my friend, Professor William Storrar, for helpful and constructive comments on a draft of this paper.
2 See, for example, Quentin Skinner, *The Foundations of Modern Political thought. Vol 2: The Age of Reformation* (Cambridge: Cambridge University Press, 1978), 302–3: 'So we find Hotman writing to Calvin in December 1558 to assure him that "everyone was pleased with your letters in which you openly indicated that you were outraged" by the inflammatory writings of Goodman and Knox.'
3 John Milbank, Catharine Pickstock and Graham Ward, eds., *Radical Orthodoxy* (London: Routledge, 1999), 2.
4 *Ibid.*
5 Sir David Lindsay, *Ane Satyre of the Thrie Estaites.* Rev. edn. (Edinburgh: Polygon, 1985).
6 Peter Matheson gives an account of similar Reformation street theatre in Berne in 1522. Its anticlericalism and adoration of Christ resulted in 'formidable transformations in patterns of deference, concepts of honour and hidden assumptions'. *The Imaginative World of the Reformation* (Edinburgh: T. & T. Clark, 2000), 5.

7 *Ane Satyre of the Thrie Estaites*, four pages from end – pages are unnumbered!
8 The similarities with the Czech Reformation are impressively explored by Jan Milič Lochman, *Zeal for Truth and Tolerance: The Ecumenical Challenge of the Czech Reformation* (Edinburgh: Scottish Academic Press, 1996), 1–4.
9 Matheson, *Imaginative World of the Reformation*, 9.
10 *Scots Confession*, Article XIV.
11 *Scots Confession*, Article XXIV.
12 John Calvin, *Institutes of the Christian Religion*, IV.xx.31.
13 See "The Appellation to the Nobility and Estates" and "The Letter to the Commonalty" in *John Knox on Rebellion*, Cambridge Texts in the History of Political Thought (ed. R. A. Mason; Cambridge: Cambridge University Press, 1994).
14 *The First Book of Discipline* (ed. with introduction and commentary by J. K. Cameron; Edinburgh: Saint Andrew Press, 1972).
15 *Scots Confession*, Article XVIII.
16 *First Book of Discipline*, 166–7.
17 On this see Donald C. Smith, *Passive Obedience and Prophetic Protest: Social Criticism in the Scottish Church, 1580–1945* (New York: Peter Lang, 1987), 11–20.
18 In "The Letter to the Commonalty" in *John Knox on Rebellion*, 118–126.
19 *Ibid.*, 124 f.
20 John Calvin, *Institutes of the Christian Religion*, III.xix.15 (trans. H. Beveridge; London: James Clarke & Co., 1949), 140.
21 *Ibid.*
22 Robert Pitcairn, ed., *The Autobiography and Diary of Mr James Melville* (Edinburgh: The Wodrow Society, 1842), 370.
23 On the development of the idea of royal supremacy in the early English Reformation, see especially Diarmid MacCulloch, *Thomas Cranmer* (New Haven: Yale University Press, 1996), esp. pp. 278, 349, 364, 576 f., 617.
24 John Cuming, ed., *The Liturgy of the Church of Scotland, or John Knox's Book of Common Order* (London: 1840), 84–5.
25 Cited from *Lex Rex* in John Coffey, *Politics, Religion and the British Revolutions: The Mind of Samuel Rutherford* (Cambridge: Cambridge University Press, 1997), 153.
26 See Coffey, *Politics, Religion and the British Revolutions*, 173.
27 The latest discussion of Rutherford on resistance is in Coffey, *Ibid.*, 175–83.
28 *Ibid.*, 170.
29 Adam Smith, *An Inquiry into the Nature and Causes of the Wealth of Nations* (ed. R. A. Campbell and A. S. Skinner; Oxford: Oxford University Press, 1976), 810.
30 *Ibid.*

31 I am indebted for these points to Professor Storrar. See also James Mackey, *Power and Christian Ethics* (Cambridge: Cambridge University Press, 1994), 121–28.

32 The least sympathetic was probably David Hume.

33 A. M. C. Waterman, *Revolution, Economics and Religion: Christian Political Economy, 1798–1833* (Cambridge: Cambridge University Press, 1991), ch. 6.

34 Cited in Hugh Watt, *New College, Edinburgh: A Centenary History* (Edinburgh: Oliver & Boyd, 1946), 3–4.

35 Boyd Hilton, *The Age of Atonement: The Influence of Evangelicalism on Social and Economic Thought, 1785–1865* (Oxford: Clarendon, 1988), 56.

36 Karl Marx, *Capital*, vol. 1 (Moscow: Progress Publishers, 1965), 617.

37 The best modern study of Chalmers is S. J. Brown, *Thomas Chalmers and the Godly Commonwealth in Scotland* (Oxford: Oxford University Press, 1982), and an incisive discussion of Chalmers' social policy is Donald Macleod, "Thomas Chalmers and Pauperism" in S. J. Brown and Michael Fry, eds., *Scotland in the Age of the Disruption* (Edinburgh: Edinburgh University Press, 1993), 63–76.

38 Thomas Chalmers, *On the Power, Wisdom and Goodness of God as Manifested in the Adaptation of External Nature to the Moral and Intellectual Constitution of Man*. Vol. 2 (London: William Pickering, 1834), 36.

39 *Ibid.*

40 *Ibid.*, 30.

41 Chalmers, *On Political Economy*, 25–6, cited in Smith, *Passive Obedience and Prophetic Protest*, 131.

42 Cited in Smith, *Ibid.*, 117.

43 Cited in Smith, *Ibid.*, 88.

44 Macleod, "Thomas Chalmers and Pauperism," 70.

45 See Smith, *Passive Obedience and Prophetic Protest*, 165, etc.

46 See S. J. Brown, "The Social Ideal of the Church of Scotland in the 1930s" in Andrew R. Morton, ed., *God's Will in a Time of Crisis: A Colloquium Celebrating the 50ᵗʰ Anniversary of the Baillie Commission* (Edinburgh: Centre for Theology and Public Issues, 1994), 14–31.

47 Alexander Gammie, *Dr George H. Morrison: The Man and His Work* (London: James Clarke, 1928), 126.

48 *Ibid.*, 134–9.

49 *Articles Declaratory of the Constitution of the Church of Scotland*, Article III.

50 On the Baillie Commission see especially, Morton, *God's Will in a Time of Crisis.*

51 Karl Barth, *The Knowledge of God and the Service of God According to the Teaching of the Reformation* (London: Hodder and Stoughton, 1938).

52 G. D. Henderson, ed., *Scots Confession, 1560 and Negative Confession, 1581* (Edinburgh: Church of Scotland, 1937).

53 See *The Biblical Doctrine of Baptism: A Study Document Issued by The Special Commission on Baptism of the Church of Scotland* (Edinburgh: Saint Andrew Press, 1958).

54 See R. S. Wallace, *Calvin's Doctrine of the Christian Life* (Edinburgh: Oliver and Boyd, 1959) and *Calvin's Doctrine of the Word and Sacrament* (Edinburgh: Oliver and Boyd, 1953), and T. F. Torrance, *Calvin's Doctrine of Man* (London: Lutterworth Press, 1949).

55 John W. de Gruchy, *Liberating Reformed Theology: A South African Contribution to an Ecumenical Debate* (Grand Rapids: Eerdmans, 1991), xii.

56 *Ibid.*, 41.

57 H. M. Kuitert, *Everything is Politics But Politics is Not Everything – A Theological Perspective on Faith and Politics* (London: SCM Press, 1986).

4

REFORMED THEOLOGY:
Whence and Whither?

ALAN P. F. SELL

The term 'Reformed theology' is slippery indeed. Some know only too well what it means – it is encapsulated in the five points of Dort, for example – and they measure all claimants to the description 'Reformed' against their chosen doctrinal criterion. Others, many Lutherans among them, profess to find the Reformed family puzzling because, in contrast to the unifying force of the Augsburg Confession, the Reformed have many confessions – indeed, in some quarters they are still writing them; and the way in which they are held varies from the most casual acknowledgement that, as it happens, these documents are part of the heritage, to sincere and lively attachment to the Helvetic, Belgic or Westminster confessions, and to the Heidelberg or Westminster catechisms. It further transpires that while some non-Reformed Christians – notably a percentage of Baptists and Anglicans – understand themselves as embracing Reformed theology, some theologians who are Reformed in terms of ecclesiastical allegiance may be far from the stricter sect of Calvin's sons and daughters. There are nowadays Reformed scholars, whether biblical or philosophical or church historical, from whose works one would not – indeed, should not – be able to infer their confessional allegiance simply because that issue is not germane to the practice of their discipline; and there are also Reformed Christians who, having imbibed certain church growth principles, hide their confessional lights under such bushels as those proclaiming 'Community Church' in order not to dissuade the sensitive or leave the childcare facilities and gymnasia, whether physical or emotional, empty.

The term 'Reformed' as descriptive of a Christian world communion is equally puzzling to many. Whether we think in terms of doctrines espoused, attitudes to Scripture, ways of worship, church order and polity, the Reformed family as it actually exists is diverse. It has spawned upholders of the penal substitutionary theory of the atonement and convinced Abelardians; biblical inerrantists and the most liberal of biblical critics; its worship is on a continuum with exclusive unaccompanied psalmody at one end and the Disney-style celebrations of the Crystal Cathedral at the other; in some parts there are ministers and deacons; in others ministers, elders and deacons; in still others, ministers, elders, deacons and doctors, to which, in Hungarian-speaking circles are added bishops. There are churches which espouse a consistorial polity, others which are congregational in government, and some in which the two styles are blended. Some Reformed churches are free churches, others are established churches, some, whether established or free, are the folk churches of their region.[1]

Confronted by such incontestable facts, Reformed Christians may be inclined to grope for some such poetic phrase as 'a richly variegated tapestry.' If, on the other hand, there existed any Reformed Christians of a cynical turn of mind, they might be tempted to wonder, 'At what point does a richly variegated tapestry become a dog's breakfast?' Rather than resorting to the wanton use of labels, I prefer to try, in a discriminating way, to ask, What are some of the factors which have brought us to our present position?

The first claim I wish to make is that there has been theological variety within the Reformed family since its inception. This is not unconnected with the fact that one of the advantages of the family is that it is not named after anyone. From the outset a variety of pastors and theologians were reflecting on the Bible in relation to their understanding of the Gospel and the circumstances in which God had placed them. Nor should we forget that 'the outset' is not a date in the sixteenth century, but encompasses the 'first Reformation' associated with such names as Valdes and Hus, to whom look back, respectively, the Waldensians of Italy and the Evangelical Church of Czech Brethren. The first Reformation emphasis upon the Sermon on the Mount and the life of Christian simplicity flowed down and mingled with the theological contributions of Zwingli, Calvin, Knox, Bucer, Farel, Bullinger, Viret, Beza and Ursinus, all of whom were singing in the same choir if not taking exactly the same part. To these we must add (to mention only the most significant) John Owen in England, Jonathan Edwards in North America, and the 'father of modern theology', Schleiermacher in Germany.

Many of these theologians were involved in drafting and publishing confessions of faith – more than sixty in the sixteenth century alone. While the early confessions display a considerable degree of unity – an unsurprising fact given the commuting between Reformed centres, and the ability of all to consult through the medium of Latin – there were significant confessional variations as time went on. The Westminster Confession's affirmation of the federal theology was suggested by contextual considerations prevailing at the time of its composition, while the Congregationalists of the Savoy Declaration (1658), who adopted the bulk of Westminster, nevertheless thought it appropriate to add a paragraph in which, over against hyper-Calvinism, they advocated the proclamation of the Gospel to all.[2] A later dispute over this latter point lasted for about two hundred years (echoes of it may be heard to this day in certain circles), and Reformed protagonists were to be found on both sides: for example, the Presbyterian turned Independent Joseph Hussey being staunchly opposed to the free offer, and Ralph Wardlaw, the Scottish Congregationalist in favour of it.[3] As for the confessions which the Reformed family has produced in the second half of the twentieth century, the term 'predestination' is generally conspicuous by its absence, and in a number of declarations the concept is not present; the Pope is no longer branded Antichrist nor the Anabaptists anathematised; and the fragility of the created order, and peace and justice are among topics which many of today's confessors, unlike their predecessors, feel bound to emphasise in their confessions.[4]

The political circumstances of the time influenced not only the directions in which the Reformed movement spread, but the ecclesiastical shape it took. With some princes and dukes opting for Lutheranism, others for the Reformed way, it would have been difficult for the Reformed in continental Europe to have escaped baptism as established church people. In any case, their experience of Anabaptists, some of whom were excitable enough, as well as of even wilder sectaries, made them psychologically unwelcoming to the free-church idea. By contrast, in England and Wales non-Anglican Reformed Christians had no option but to work out their polity in face of an establishment which, to the early Separatists, spoke of nothing so clearly as Antichrist, and which to their less threatened successors seemed nevertheless to be a compromised church, having one foot in Scripture, the other in a particular national constitution.

Among many social influences upon the Reformed tradition to which one might point are the changing ideas concerning slavery in the nineteenth century, and concerning women in the later nineteenth and twentieth centuries. Thus far Reformed churches have universally embraced the former, whereas a continuing witness needs to be made to a number of Reformed churches regarding the latter. In both cases the Reformed, like other Christians, have found themselves having to catch up with the Gospel according to which all are one in Christ; and their theologies – especially their doctrines of the Church and the ministry – have had to be revised.[5]

Time would fail even to scratch the surface of the many factors in the intellectual environment which have resulted in theological adjustment. I think, for example, of a positive benefit of the Enlightenment – a phenomenon too easily lambasted by some theologians today who forget that God can work through Cyrus. We owe to the deists among others that protest in the interests of morality against God presented as a wrathful Father who could not be merciful until he had killed his obedient Son. Thus Thomas Paine refers to 'the outrage offered to the moral justice of God by supposing him to make the innocent suffer for the guilty, and the loose morality and low contrivance of supposing him to change himself into the shape of a man in order to make an excuse to himself for not executing his supposed sentence on Adam.'[6] It is not fanciful to suppose that McLeod's Campbell's insistence in *The Nature of the Atonement* (1856) that the first word of the Gospel is grace is at least an implicit endorsement of such charges, as well as a more general impetus towards the later nineteenth-century emphasis upon the Fatherhood of God which, when in some circles it was running out into a bland humanism, was corrected by P. T. Forsyth and others with the insistence that it is holy Fatherhood with which we have to do.[7]

The Romantic movement's influence, especially when coupled with post-Hegelian immanentist thought, likewise prompted significant changes in the formulation of Reformed theology. We may recall, for example, the Mercersburg theology of John Williamson Nevin and Philip Schaff, which did well to remind those who needed to be reminded that the Reformed share in the entire catholic heritage of Christian faith, and that the witness did not fizzle out at the end of the New Testament to be rekindled only at the Reformation;[8] but which tended to emphasise the organic model, the idea of continuity and the doctrine of the Incarnation to such an extent that sinful humanity's rescue at the Cross seemed to J. H. A. Bomberger and others in the German Reformed Church to be played down in a quite un-Pauline way.[9]

The rise of modern biblical scholarship was a further significant factor for theology at large, and for Reformed theology, with its formal elevation of the Bible as the supreme rule of faith and order, in particular. On the one hand it yielded the so-called Princetonian scholastics – Charles Hodge and Archibald Alexander, debtors to Turretin's *Institutio Theologiae Elencticae*, in which was propounded a doctrine of biblical inerrancy according to which the Bible is inerrant not only where doctrinal or moral matters are concerned, but also regarding 'statements of facts, whether scientific, historical, or geographical.'[10] Later versions of this theory, powerful to this day in some quarters, have been a ground of more than one inner-Reformed secession. On the other hand the new approach to Scripture yielded Robert Mackintosh, that delightfully sardonic self-styled refugee from the Free Church of Scotland to Congregationalism who, in a pamphlet provocatively entitled *The Obsoleteness of the Westminster Confession of Faith*, made merry with the proof texts which the Westminster divines were required to supply after the confession was completed. At the end of a splendidly teasing paragraph he writes, 'Finally – and I specially recommend this to supporters of the Establishment principle – the proof that the civil magistrate may lawfully summon religious synods is found in the fact that Herod consulted the chief priests in order to plot more successfully how to murder the infant Jesus. Comment on these citations could be nothing but a feeble anti-climax. Let us treasure them up in our hearts.'[11]

Coming closer to our own time I simply list the way in which some have followed Barth, others Brunner on the issue of natural theology; the embracing by some theologians of the principles of process thought; the several contextual theologies – black, liberation, feminist, Minjung; the growth of conservative evangelical theology; and the concern of many for a theology of religions: all of these have, severally or in combination, been embraced by Reformed theologians among others, and as a result re-castings of Reformed theological positions, ranging from the subtle to the violent, have been proposed. So much, very sketchily, for the 'Whence' of my title. What, now, of the 'Whither'? I shall make three points each of which encompasses a positive declaration and one or more cautionary words.

I

First, as we go forward we should do well to remember that Reformed theology is catholic in intention, but ever at risk of affording hospitality to the sectarian demon. A moment ago I spoke of re-castings of Reformed theological positions. But what are these positions? Whatever they are, they are not positions which are exclusively the possession of the Reformed. For Reformed theology is catholic in intention. The Reformers did not set out to devise novel sets of doctrines, or to invent new churches. Rather their objective was to reform the one Church according to the Word of God. The unity of the Church is God's gift to his people.[12] It is the possession of those who are, 'in Christ,' who 'abide in Christ,' who are branches of the vine, saints by calling, limbs of the body of Christ, members of the household of faith, the priesthood of believers.[13] The classical Reformed confessions bear witness to this fact, and Dr. Krafft summed up their testimony in a paper submitted to the First General Presbyterian Council in these terms:

> We acknowledge and confess one Catholic or Universal Church, which is a communion of all believers, who look for their whole salvation in Jesus Christ alone, who are cleansed by his blood, and sanctified by his Spirit; that his holy Church is confined to no special place, or limited to special persons, but is scattered over the whole earth, and yet is united in one and the same spirit by the power of faith.[14]

I should myself prefer to say that the Church is united by the grace and calling of God, to which our faith is the enabled response; and I miss here a reference to the Church triumphant in heaven. But that the Reformed have traditionally conceived of the Church as catholic is quite clear. Turning to our own century, we find that the same point is made in *A Declaration of Faith* (1967) of the Congregational Church in England and Wales:

> We worship God through Jesus Christ within the Christian Church. This Church is the whole company of believers, drawn from all humanity irrespective of nation, colour, race or language ... The Church is founded upon Jesus Christ ... God creates the Church to be one, holy, catholic and apostolic ...[15]

To say that the Reformed affirm the catholicity of the Church does not mean that there are no doctrinal emphases which the Reformed have traditionally wished to make.[16] Over and above their witness to the general Reformation watchwords, Grace alone, Faith alone, Christ alone, Scripture alone, the Reformed have emphasised the initiative of God and the work of the Spirit in salvation, the sovereignty and providence of God, the inescapability of the Church and the necessity of its right ordering, the true presence of Christ at his Supper, and the work of the exalted Christ as prophet, priest and king. But they have propounded these teachings not because they believed that they were in some exclusive sense Reformed, but because they regarded them as important, and in some quarters overlooked, aspects of catholic truth given in Scripture.

To return for a moment to the Congregationalists of 1967: having affirmed the catholicity of the Church, they go on at once to say that 'the Church as Christians know it is not yet as God would have it be ...'.[17] Such statements of the obvious have not always characterised Reformed confessions, but they are none the less true. The empirical Church, as is well known, is riddled by sectarian division; we do not appear to be, in Paul's words, 'one person in Christ Jesus.'[18] The question of the degree of doctrinal or ethical tolerance properly to be allowed within the Church is one which has perplexed the Church in every generation; friction has been caused, parties have been formed, secessions have taken place. For their part the Reformed in various times and places have not been slow to detect the sectarian spirit in Christians of other traditions. If the Pope thinks that he must not accept invitations to the Lord's Table in our churches, we say that is because he espouses a sectarian doctrine of ministry and sacraments; if a high Anglican ecumenical drafter proposes a fudge which will enable those who wish to believe that re-ordination is occurring when the overall desire is to reconcile ministries, we say that he is a sectarian; if a Strict and Particular Baptist bars us from communion because we have not been immersed, we say the same thing. How easy it is to see when others are being sectarian!

The sad truth is that the Reformed harbour a sectarian demon in their own bosom. Our history is full of examples of inner-family division. Time would fail me to tell of the Relief Church, the Reformed Presbyterians, the Old Light Burghers, the New Light Burghers, the Old Light Antiburghers and the New Light Antiburghers, all of whom, together with those who departed during the 'lifter' controversy of 1783, were separately active in Scotland during the eighteenth century; and it is almost impossible to keep up with the Presbyterians of South Korea who, when last I enquired, were to be found in approximately one hundred denominations. It is also true that within the Reformed family there have been occasions of ecclesiastical healing, and there are even some trans-confessional unions in which those of the Reformed heritage share. Neither do I deny that very often those who have led secessions have been in effect, and sometimes quite vociferously, passing judgement upon a church deemed to have gone off the doctrinal rails or fallen into non-evangelistic slumber. But there have also been occasions when the sectarian spirit, which unchurches those who do not adhere to our way of expressing the truth, has prevailed. Not indeed that secession is the necessary consequence of the sectarian spirit: in a way it is more painful when it is not. Thus, in our own time we have caucuses and politicised pressure groups within churches which can seem on occasion to elevate their particular way of doing theology, or their preferred set of ethical stances above the Gospel which has made us one, so that if we do not all look exactly up their periscope we are somehow traitors to the cause or less than *bona fide* believers. This is the Galatian heresy, and it is sad.[19] It is my conviction that our favoured ways of worship, our church polities, our doctrinal convictions, and our ethical stances may not be raised to the position of principles on the basis of which we exclude from fellowship any who sincerely confess the Lordship of Christ. So to wield them would be legalistically to elevate our customs, formulae and behaviour above the Gospel of God's grace, and to divide those whom God has already made one in Christ.

Where the Reformed sectarian prescribing of doctrine is concerned I often feel that if those who claimed to stand to strongly by the confessions would only read some of the prefaces to the confessions, where the authors profess themselves open to change if any can show how they have departed from Scripture, they would understand that even the authors realised that they were *interpreting* Scripture – what else could they do? What else can any of us do? Again, there is a moral in the way God teased his Presbyterians of Old Dissent in England and Wales during the eighteenth century. For a variety of reasons – the fact that their forebears had been the majority party among those who compiled the Westminster Confession notwithstanding – most of them had become Unitarian by the century's close.[20] To repeat, when once we fall into the trap of thinking that people are saved by adherence to our confessional formulae, or that confessions as such guard the faith, we have left saving grace behind, and have fallen into a new legalism; and if on this basis we proceed to unchurch others, or withhold fellowship from them, we have adopted a posture which is clearly sectarian in spirit and in result. For making this point so strongly, some of the Arian Presbyterian divines of the eighteenth century, so frequently maligned for their doctrinal conclusions, deserve our gratitude. Said one of them, John Taylor of Norwich, 'a popish, anti-Christian Spirit I will ever oppose, as God shall enable me'[21] – and he said it not against Rome, but in opposition to the Independent James Sloss of Castle Gate Church, Nottingham, who wished a church member, Joseph Rawson, who was accused of consorting with 'heretics,' to answer a test question couched in orthodox Trinitarian terms. Rawson replied in biblical terms, but this was deemed insufficient, so the church meeting banished him from the Lord's Table. When he resolved to present himself at communion in any case he was threatened with civil action. John Taylor rose in defence of freedom of conscience and in opposition to the 'popish' imposition by dissenters of credal tests.[22]

But even if we take the point concerning the peril of elevating our formulae above the Gospel, we are not yet out of the wood. The following words of the Unitarian Joseph Priestley will help me to make the point. He writes in 1783:

> ... though the *Calvinistic Dissenters* are frequently losing the younger, the more thoughtful and inquisitive part of their congregations, numbers of the more illiterate people are continually joining them; and societies of *Calvinistic Baptists* are readily formed, and easily extend themselves; so that of late years their numbers are very considerably increased. This is, in some measure, owing to the zeal of those who hold such tenets; a zeal which is easily accounted for, from the stress which they have been led to lay upon them; imagining that men's future happiness depends upon their holding the right faith: whereas the *Rational Dissenters* do not think that the future state of any man will depend upon his opinions, but only on his disposition of mind and his conduct of life. They have, therefore, naturally less zeal for all matters of opinion than the Calvinists have, and for the same reason they are less solicitous about making converts.[23]

To the extent that Priestley challenges those who think that salvation comes to others when their own set of tenets, expressed in their way, is embraced, he underlines the point I have been trying to make. But when he says that a person's future state turns upon disposition of mind and conduct of life, he might seem to be sitting light to the question of truth. Does it matter what we believe so long as we are of a pleasing mental disposition and act morally? Priestley, of course, thinks it does matter greatly: not for nothing did he resent the way in which some were lumping Unitarians together with deists. But he could more easily assume widespread faith in God and the desirability of commitment to Jesus (however understood) than we can. Hence for us his words taken just as they stand, when transposed into our present-day context, pose clamantly the question of truth.

I conclude this section with two further remarks to make concerning Reformed catholicity. First, when we articulate our catholic theology in dialogue with Christian traditions other than our own we frequently find that a helpful way of approaching classical doctrinal disputes is to ask, 'In expressing things as they did, what were the "other side" trying to guard against?' Thus, for example, the evangelical Arminians of the eighteenth century stoutly opposed a Calvinist scholasticism according to which human salvation was resolved into a matter of God's eternal, inscrutable will. Where is grace? they properly enquired. Positively, they wished to assert the importance of the human being's free response to that same grace. On the other hand, the Calvinists wished to exalt God's sovereignty in salvation, and loathed any position which seemed to suggest that God cannot quite save us unless we give him permission, or otherwise assist by an act of decision. The international Reformed-Methodist dialogue commission concluded that both had a point, that the dire perils perceived on both sides were rightly to be avoided, and that this hoary dispute, while people may still sincerely take up either side of it, should no longer be regarded as church dividing. The commission's report declares that 'we have found that the classical doctrinal issues we were asked to review ought not to be seen as obstacles to unity between Methodists and Reformed.'[24] Two other international dialogues between the Reformed and others have reached similar conclusions following the discussion of hitherto neuralgic issues. That with the Lutherans, building upon earlier consultations in Europe and the United States declares that 'nothing stands in the way of church fellowship,' and that, accordingly, the way is clear for 'full pulpit and altar/table fellowship, with necessary mutual recognition of ministers ordained for word and sacrament';[25] while that with the Disciples of Christ affirms that 'there are no theological or ecclesiological issues which need divide us as churches.'[26] These developments, I suggest, ought to mean that when in the future systematic theologies are written by Reformed, Lutherans, Methodists and Disciples, account is taken of the positions reached. It too frequently happens that systematicians proceed in apparent ignorance of doctrinal steps taken by the traditions to which they belong. For example, we might expect that henceforth Disciples theologians will write ecclesiology in the light of the agreement that there can (and do) exist church orders in which both *paedobaptism* and believers' baptism are alternatively available.[27] Even if theologians should wish to protest that official dialogue reports of the kind to which I have referred have moral authority only, they ought at least to acknowledge their existence, expound their contents, and present grounds for disagreeing with them if that is their desire.

II

Secondly, by way of summary, I should like to quote my own attempted definition of catholicity:

> On the ground of the finished work of Christ the Son, the Father graciously and freely calls out by his Spirit a people for his praise and service; he enables their confession of Christ's Lordship and, in drawing them to himself, he gives them to one another in a fellowship in which all barriers of race, sex and class have been broken down; this people, whose membership encompasses heaven and earth, we call the Church catholic.[28]

My second affirmation is that as we go forward we should remember that Reformed theology has a comprehensive sweep in principle and manifests certain lacunae in practice. That is to say, the theological vision embraces the whole of life, whilst at the same time manifesting certain blind spots. I shall attempt to illustrate this claim by reference to practical theology, ethics and apologetics.

It is supremely in the practice of the liturgy of Word and sacrament that theology is anchored for the people of God as a whole. Here the Word is proclaimed in such a way that its claim on the whole of life is made plain; here sinners who are also saints by calling adjust their sights to the challenge of God's holy love, and, by the Spirit's help, resolve to amend their ways and engage with enthusiasm in God's mission. Here the saints offer praise and thanksgiving to the One who has so loved them. Even from this brief and incomplete statement of principle concerning worship as the *locus* of theology we can see that, for good or ill, what actually takes place in worship itself makes a theological statement.[29] Is the emphasis more upon sin than upon grace? Does the Good News which is proclaimed tell of an atonement which is open to us because it has first met the needs of God, or are we (perhaps sentimentally) led to think that the Cross concerns humanity – even me – alone? Is Christ presented primarily as teacher, master, elder brother, or saviour? Will the congregation perceive that the primary objective is to bring them into the presence of the holy one, or will they think that it is to make them feel good? Are the prayers the prayers of the people, or of the pastor? Do the hymns, taken altogether, tend in the direction of praising God or coddling us? Over the course of the weeks do we feel that we are being nurtured in holy living, equipped for mission, and prepared to face the issues of life – including death? Or is death something mentioned only at funeral services – by which time it is too late for the deceased? So one might go on; but enough has been said to indicate that as the gathering of the people under the Word of God, worship is a theological *locus*; and also that the content of worship, and the manner in which it is conducted together make a theological statement.[30]

I wish to pursue a little further a point I have just made – the one concerning the equipping of the saints for what used to be called a godly walk. My limited experience suggests that on the one hand many are craving for serenity, seeking guidance for life, desirous of 'finding themselves.' Hence courses on spirituality, the popularity of counselling sessions, and the like, many of which are quite unrelated to Christian theology (I do not adversely judge them, I simply state a fact). On the other hand we have the mushrooming of seminary courses in practical theology, many of which seem to be more practical than theological. I do not deny the usefulness of some of these. Depending upon one's context it may be very important to know something about survival techniques in the jungle; or how to create a website for your church; or (though this is not a problem which perplexes many British ministers) how to electronically tag the church's children lest they get lost on, or are illicitly enticed from, the church campus. Again, it can be informative and instructive – even at times necessary, to reflect upon the impact of Romanticism on nineteenth-century hymnody, or to inquire into the doctrine of humanity which is presupposed by the counselling techniques of Carl Rogers.

My point is that, perhaps aided and abetted by ideas concerning the professionalization of the ministry, the mushrooming and modularization of theological courses, and the laicizing of theological education, there is in many quarters – not least Reformed ones – a bifurcation between systematic-cum-doctrinal theology and practical theology. Similarly, there has grown up a bifurcation between systematic-cum-doctrinal theology and Christian ethics. As far as I have been able to discover the latter began in England in the eighteenth century, when Henry Grove, the dissenting academy tutor at Taunton, separated ethics from dogmatics in the curriculum of the academy.[31] In view of such current pressing issues as Third World debt, genetic engineering and the like, it is not surprising that there is intense and frequently highly-specialized activity in the field of applied ethics sometimes at the expense of consideration of the presuppositions of Christian ethics and of the analysis of the logic of Christian ethical utterance.[32] But ought not the Reformed ideals of theological comprehensiveness and a Gospel for the whole of life prompt us to query such bifurcations at the level of underlying principle? Certainly within our own tradition – especially in the Puritan parts of it – we have some models to challenge and help us. It is quite clear that when the Puritans and those in their tradition wrote their bodies of practical divinity, they were under no illusion that they were writing manuals on how to shoe a horse, helpful though such knowledge may have been. Rather, in many cases the same divines who could see off Arminianism or antinomianism or Socinianism or deism to their own satisfaction could also offer such works as *A Lifting up for the Downcast* (William Bridge, 1648), *Precious Remedies against Satan's Devices* (Thomas Brooks, 1652), and *The Saint's Everlasting Rest* (1650). The last, by the seventeenth century's Reformed pastor *par excellence*, Richard Baxter, epitomises the seamless robe of biblical-cum-doctrinal-cum-pastoral theology. These divines could encourage the saint, reprove the sinner, handle topics such as guilt and assurance, and write at length on the nature of, and resources for, the godly walk. Of course they did not have to reckon with modern biblical criticism. They could make assumptions which we no longer can. But the questions press: Have we lost the skill? Have we lost the language? Have we lost the experiences? To the extent that we have lost these, does it matter? I suggest that it does if it is the theologian's task to be first a servant of the Word of God and secondly one who can encourage the saints to live their lives in the presence of God.

But as well as loving God with heart and soul and strength, Christians are challenged to love him with all their mind. In the nineteenth century the Reformed were to the fore in Christian apologetics – not least in Scotland. Flint, Bruce, Iverach, Orr – these are just a few of the theologians who were engaged in coming to terms with agnosticism, materialism, naturalism, evolutionary thought, and idealistic philosophy, and all against the background of modern biblical criticism and the devastation by Hume and Kant of the classical theistic arguments.[33] I have elsewhere gauged the swift demise of such apologetic activity by reference to the concerns of the World Presbyterian Alliance and the International Congregational Council (the forebears of the World Alliance of Reformed Churches, 1970) as expressed in their proceedings and other literature. Until about 1920 they frequently discussed their theology in relation to the intellectual climate of the day, but since that time this theme has been conspicuous by its absence from the literature.[34] It is partly that we are unsure where to start with those beyond our circles who are still sufficiently interested to ask for a reason for our hope. But it is partly that some of our giants have been telling us that the effort should not be made – cannot be made, with which conclusion, though on quite different grounds, many postmodernists are in hearty accord. At the heart of the problem is the question of starting points. For example (and here I must plead brevity as the excuse for crudity), if, as with Butler against the deists, we occupy the rationalistic ground of our opponents we shall not – as Butler himself fully realised[35] – be able to introduce certain considerations which are germane, even vital, to Christian faith. On the other hand, if we allow ourselves to become imprisoned in what has been called the circle of revelation, how shall we get out of it to meet enquirers at all? Is there what Mr. Tony Blair might call a third way? I very much hope so, not least because, in my now rather lengthy experience as an homiletic vagrant I find time and again that many of those still in the pews have questions concerning the faith which trouble them, and which they feel they cannot – or dare not – articulate either because they pick up no clues to suggest that their questions would receive adequate attention, or because they fear being slapped down by the godly on the ground of their alleged faithlessness. But not to address the honest intellectual concerns of the church member is a failure in *practical* theology; not to address the honest intellectual concerns of 'outside' critics whether hostile or benign, is a failure in mission. Not to consider the question of common ground – whether epistemological or ethical – on which we can stand with those who do not share our faith is a failure in ecumenism, the objective of which is the whole inhabited earth giving glory to God. I do not say that every Christian is competent to rise to the more technical aspects of these tasks – to say this is not to be elitist in a nasty sense, it is simply to recognize that there are diversities of gifts; but it would be reassuring to feel that church members might know who can handle such matters, just as they might know who has a pastoral ear, who can sing a solo, who can teach the young, who is good at flower arranging, who can maintain the churchyard; and it would be even more reassuring to feel that every church member felt able, when the opportunity arose, to speak with confidence, joy and humility of the things he or she has seen and heard.

Just as Calvin sought a Geneva reformed according to the Word of God, so many Reformed theologians properly emphasize that the eschatological vision is of the whole inhabited earth glorifying God. Accordingly, they heed their several contexts, they advocate the cause of the poor and the down-trodden, they seek justice for all and devote themselves to pressing ethical issues. If I am brief at this point it is simply because this kind of activity is not something to which we need to be recalled. I would simply utter the cautionary word that one of the ways of ensuring the rootage of such activity in the Gospel is to ask from time to time the questions, What do we do or say that right-minded humanists do not? Are our motivations identical with those of the Ethical Society? This is not to deny that we should, where issues of peace, justice, human need and the like are concerned, stand together with those whose beliefs may differ from our own. It is simply to invite Christians to reflect upon the ground and inspiration of their witness, and to relate their social action to their worship. As Nicholas Wolterstorff has written,

> It is because our fellow human beings are joined irrevocably with us in mirroring God's glory, especially God's wisdom and goodness, that we are to treat them with justice. But it is also God's glory, including God's wisdom and goodness, that grounds our worship with praise and adoration and blessing and thanksgiving. Worship and justice are thus joined in being two ways of acknowledging God's glory. So united are they, that to worship and not practice justice is to worship inauthentically ... and to practice justice and not worship is to practice justice inauthentically, or in blindness to God's glory all about us.[36]

III

So to my third and final claim: as we go forward we should take full account of the fact that the Reformed have a theological method which is integrally related to their pneumatology and to their *completed* ecclesiology, but which is open to abuse in more than one way. The positive thesis is that at our best the Reformed have understood that the Word of God, which is addressed to the people of God, is discerned by the Spirit through the Bible within the fellowship of the Church. In this context 'the Church' embraces both the local fellowship and the heritage of faith to which it is heir.

In two directions at least that principle is vulnerable. First, in the course of our history wedges have sometimes been driven between Spirit, Bible and Church in such a way that we have spawned individualistic spirituals on the one hand and biblical fundamentalists on the other – neither of whom, have much of an eye to the fellowship as corporate hearer and student of God's Word. Secondly, in practice it has too frequently been only a part of the Church which has assumed the right to, or been expected to, discern the Word. With this I come to the explanation of my term 'completed ecclesiology': I do believe that through their study of the Bible in the context of their political situation, the English and Welsh orthodox Dissenters and their American heirs completed the polity of the Reformed tradition by embracing the whole people of God in the priestly governance of the body. Calvin, that is to say, left matters hanging with the elders and deacons; the Congregationalists and Particular Baptists rooted the polity in the whole people of God.[37] Hence the importance of Church Meeting, where, under the leadership of the one called to minister the Word and sacraments, the saints gather to acknowledge the Lordship of Christ over the entire life and witness of the church, and to seek unanimity (not majority rule) in him. There are problems here, of course. It is possible for the local churches to become isolationist and to elevate autonomy above the Gospel. But all church polities have their pitfalls – there can be heretical bishops, recalcitrant presbyteries and ungodly church meetings. But at their best these Calvinist-Puritan spirits knew that to be a member of the Church catholic is to be anchored as a member among the saints in a given place. Clearly, the polity turns upon knowing who the saints are. This has implications for ecclesiastical discipline – in many places today a lost art; but it also presupposes that there is a distinction of eternal significance between those who are in Christ and those who are not.[38] Is this something which we still wish to maintain, or ought to maintain? Again, the polity implies an adverse criticism not only of the polity of the established Church of England but of continental Reformed state church polities as well. In a word, it is critical of lingering Constantinianism. While maintaining that church and state have mutual obligations towards one another, it will not confuse their respective powers or suppose that the state can determine the worship, ordering and witness of the church.[39] It cannot equate the concept of catholicity with that of ecclesiastical monopolism within a state. And it cannot allow that one becomes a Christian – still less one of a particular brand – simply by virtue of being born in a particular place. There are matters here which need urgent attention within the Reformed family, especially if we wish realistically to claim that ministry is the task of the whole people of God – that is, of the people of God as Church,[40] and not just as individuals each shining in his or her corner and offering his or her talent; and if we believe, as I do, that theologizing is too important to be left to the theologians who, perhaps more than most, need the checks and balances supplied by the fellowship of saints. Moreover, if the Reformation was in part a protest against the people's having religion done to them by the priests, it is a poor exchange if in our circles they now have it done to them by the presbyteries – or even by autocratic 'princes of the pulpit.' Note that in none of this do I employ the language of democracy in the sense of 'one person, one vote' and government by the majority. My concern is with the lordship of Christ in his Church, and with the mutuality of *episcope* as between the several *foci* of churchly life.[41]

From the membership of the Church we may continue to hope and pray that there will be raised up those who shall teach the flock and educate the ministry. I cannot here embark upon the question of theological education,[42] but I should like to say that in addition to theological competence, professional theologians need two further things. First, the understanding that, as Forsyth put it, the theologian 'represents the rights of the laity. He defends their only *locus standi*. He stakes Christianity on something that can be verified not indeed by human nature, or by natural religion, but by a universal experience of grace, where preacher and theologian are all laymen, yet all experts, alike.'[43] Secondly, if theologians are to give God glory in their work – and this, I repeat, should be the primary objective of Reformed theologians – we need that humility which understands that we can take no credit for our message: we have received it as a gift of grace. Neither can we tie all the loose ends or devise the absolutely copper-bottomed theological system; for what we have received has come from One whose nature and love far surpass our powers of comprehension. Yet again, we see that theology is a great leveller. Which brings me back to where I started: Reformed theology is concerned with catholic truth; to this I now add that the students and practitioners of it are the Church catholic.

IV

Whence Reformed theology? I have attempted briefly to remind you of the diversity of the Reformed family's theological roots, and of the many ways in which our theological and doctrinal positions have been articulated in relation to political, social, intellectual and other influences. To such influences Reformed theologians have responded positively, or negatively, and with, or sometimes without, due discrimination.

Whither Reformed theology? It would be foolish to deny that there have been doctrinal emphases which have characterised the Reformed family, but I have suggested that in intention Reformed theology is catholic. At the same time our history is riddled with sectarianism which has frequently led to inner-family secessions. But the catholicity of our doctrines and of our ecclesiology ought to prompt us to work for the healing of the one body of Christ, ever remembering that ecumenism, like charity, begins at home. Furthermore, we ought, when doing our theological-ecumenical work, to draw upon those doctrinal accords which have been attained.

I next sought to show that, consistently with the comprehensive sweep of Reformed theology, Reformed theologians might give more thought in the future to the Church's worship as a theological *locus*, and to the content and manner of worship as making a theological statement. Against this background further reflection might follow on the presuppositions of that godly living which is a response to the Gospel of God's grace, and on those apologetic questions which clamour for attention if we are to love God with all our mind. In both cases the question of common ground with those who do not hold our faith is clamantly raised.

Finally, I suggested that the Reformed have a theological method which is integrally related to their pneumatology and ecclesiology. It turns upon the conviction that we discern the mind of God (insofar as we do discern it) by the Spirit, through the Scriptures, within the fellowship of the Church. We are challenged, I think, to reflect further on this method; but, more importantly, to practise it. This means that we shall ensure that our polity facilitates the ministry of the whole people of God, a significant part of which ought to be their theologizing. In this connection I believe that the established church idea which is found in some parts of the Reformed family is a dissuasive, whereas the Congregational idea, properly practised and fertilized by consistorial arrangements adopted because they are right and not simply because they are useful, is a decided advantage. But the latter throws into relief the question, Who are the Church? When we think we know who they are, we can be waylaid into a falsely pietistic, isolationist ghetto; on the other hand, if we do not know who they are we face the possibility that the church has become so identified with the society in which it lives that it is quite unable to be either a witness or a prophet to it.

So much for some of the things Reformed theologians might be pondering in the coming years. As to the manner of our theologizing, allow me in conclusion to quote myself a second time:

It is no bad thing for the Reformed, whose path has been strewn with intellectual battles within and without, to recall that the Bible says more about letting our light shine than about keeping our pencils sharp. No doubt the Reformed will ever wish to attend to the latter as a means to the former, but let them beware of sharp pencils and dim lights.[44]

Notes

1 On Reformed variety see further, Alan P. F. Sell, "The Reformed Family Today: Some Theological Reflections," in *Major Themes in the Reformed Tradition* (ed. Donald K. McKim; Grand Rapids: Eerdmanns, 1992), 433–41. For empirical evidence see Jean-Jaques Bauswein and Lukas Vischer, eds., *The Reformed Family Worldwide* (Grand Rapids: Eerdmanns, 1999).

2 A. G. Matthews, ed., *The Savoy Declaration of Faith and Order* (London: Independent Press, 1959), ch. 20.

3 See Joseph Hussey, *God's Operations of Grace But No Offers of Grace* (1707); Ralph Wardlaw, *Systematic Theology* (ed. James R. Campbell, 1857), II.549. For this and related matters see Alan P. F. Sell, *The Great Debate: Calvinism, Arminianism and Salvation* (Eugene, Or.: Wipf & Stock, 1998).

4 See further Arthur C. Cochrane, *Reformed Confessions of the 16th Century* (Philadelphia: Westminster Press, 1966); Lukas Vischer, ed., *Reformed Witness Today* (Bern: Evangelische Arbeitsstelle Cekumene Schweiz, 1982); Alasdair I. C. Heron, *The Westminster Confession in the Church Today* (Edinburgh: Saint Andrew Press, 1982).

5 It is only fair to point out that a number of the Reformed churches which do not yet ordain women are inhibited by cultural rather than biblical or theological considerations. This does not, of course, alleviate the pain of those women who, in the churches concerned, feel called to ministry. Some of these churches have yet to reach their centuries. It ill behoves us, who took nineteen-hundred years to brace ourselves to ordain women to wax too impatient with our friends, though we ought continually to encourage them to see what we have belatedly tumbled to.

6 Thomas Paine, *The Age of Reason* (1794–1807; repr. London: Watts, 1938), 35.

7 For Campbell see G. M. Tuttle, *So Rich a Soil: John McLeod Campbell on Christian Atonement* (Edinburgh: The Handsel Press, 1986). For Forsyth see Trevor Hart, ed., *Justice the True and Only Mercy: Essays on the Life and Theology of Peter Taylor Forsyth* (Edinburgh: T. & T. Clark, 1995); Alan P. F. Sell, ed., *P. T. Forsyth, Theologian for a New Millennium* (London: The United Reformed Church, 1999).

8 I like to think that this lesson has largely been learned, though as late as 1957 the philosopher and Anglican H. A. Hodges could write of the English Free Churches that among them 'there is no real awareness of anything in Christian history or tradition that is earlier than the sixteenth century.' See his *Anglicanism and Orthodoxy: A Study in Dialectical Churchmanship* (London: SCM Press, 1957), 29. The charge was too sweeping even when he wrote it.

9 See further, Alan P. F. Sell, *Commemorations: Studies in Christian Thought and History* (Calgary: University of Calgary Press and Cardiff: University of Wales Press, 1993; Eugene, Or.: Wipf & Stock, 1998), ch. 11.

10 Charles Hodge, *Systematic Theology* (New York: Scribners, 1871), 1.163.

11 Robert Mackintosh, *The Obsoleteness of the Westminster Confession of Faith,* bound with his *Essays Towards a New Theology* (Glasgow: Maclehose, 1889), 48. I am pleased to observe that some years after I attempted a 'resurrection' for Mackintosh (*Robert Mackintosh: Theologian of Integrity,* Bern: Peter Lang, 1977), his works are beginning to be cited by other scholars – for example by Dale A. Johnson, *The Changing Shape of English Nonconformity, 1825–1925* (New York: OUP, 1999).

12 See further, Alan P. F. Sell, "Reformed Identity: A Non-issue of Catholic Significance," *Reformed Review,* forthcoming; *idem, A Reformed, Evangelical, Catholic Theology: The Contribution of the World Alliance of Reformed Churches, 1875–1982* (Grand Rapids: Eerdmans, 1991), ch. 3.

13 2 Cor 5:19; John 15:5; Rom 1:7; 1 Cor 12:27; Gal 6:10; Eph 2:19; 1 Pet 2:5, 9.

14 Report of the Proceedings of the First General Presbyterian Council (Edinburgh: Thomas and Archibald Constable, 1877), 46.

15 *A Declaration of Faith* (London: Congregational Church in England and Wales, 1967), 26–7.

16 See further, for example, John H. Leith, *Introduction to the Reformed Tradition: A Way of Being the Christian Community* (Richmond, Va.: John Knox Press, 1977); Donald K. McKim, 'The "heart and center" of the Reformed Faith,' *Reformed Review* LI no. 3 (Spring 1988): 206–19.

17 *A Declaration of Faith*, 27.

18 Gal 3:28.

19 See further, Alan P. F. Sell, *Aspects of Christian Integrity*, ch. 4; *idem*, *Commemorations*, ch. 2; "Reformed Identity."

20 For an attempt to tell this complicated tale see Alan P. F. Sell, *Dissenting Thought and the Life of the Churches: Studies in an English Tradition* (San Francisco: Edwin Mellen Press, 1990), ch. 5.

21 John Taylor, *A Further Defence of the Common Rights of Christians* (1738), 78.

22 See further, Sell, *Dissenting Thought*, ch. 7.

23 *The Theological and Miscellaneous Works of Joseph Priestley*, ed. J. T. Rutt (1817–31), XXI.480.

24 *Reformed and Methodists in Dialogue: Report of the Reformed/Methodist Conversations in 1985 and 1987* (Geneva: World Alliance of Reformed Churches, 1988), 14. Among other papers contributed to these conversations are Geoffrey Wainwright, "Perfect salvation in the teaching of Wesley and Calvin," in *idem*, *Methodists in Dialog* (Nashville: Kingswood Books, 1995), ch. 8; Alan P. F. Sell, "Some reflections on Reformed-Methodist relations," in *idem*, *Dissenting Thought and the Life of the Churches*, ch. 21.

25 *Toward Church Fellowship: Report of the Joint Commission of the Lutheran World Federation and the World Alliance of Reformed Churches* (Geneva: LWF and WARC, 1989), 28.

26 *Towards Closer Fellowship* (Geneva: World Alliance of Reformed Churches, 1988), 14.

27 The international Baptist-Reformed dialogue invited the members of the Baptist World Alliance of Reformed Churches to consider the possibility of such an order, grounded in a fresh understanding of the *process* of Christian initiation. See *Baptists and Reformed in Dialogue* (Geneva: WARC, 1984); Sell, *A Reformed, Evangelical, Catholic Theology*, 142–46.

28 Sell, "Reformed identity."

29 So too, does the architectural setting of worship where one of the challenges is to design and construct buildings which at one and the same time speak of the 'high and holy' one, and of the God in the midst of his people. Not, indeed, that there can be no worship without special buildings. But if we build the buildings they will 'say' something, and it is well that it is something which undergirds our theology.

30 See further, Sell, *Aspects of Christian Integrity*, 142 ff.

31 See Sell, *Dissenting Thought*, ch. 6.

32 See Alan. P. F. Sell, 'A renewed plea for "impractical" divinity,' *Studies in Christian Ethics* VIII (1995): 68–91.

33 See Alan P. F. Sell, *Defending and Declaring the Faith: Some Scottish Examples, 1860–1920* (Exeter: Paternoster Press and Colorado Springs: Helmers & Howard, 1987).

34 See Sell, *A Reformed, Evangelical, Catholic Theology*, ch. 5 – the shortest main chapter.

35 Joseph Butler, *The Analogy of Religion* (1736), London: Ward Lock, n.d., 192.

36 Nicholas Wolterstorff, "Worship and Justice," reprinted in McKim, *Major Themes in the Reformed Tradition,* 316.

37 See Alan P. F. Sell, *Saints: Visible, Orderly and Catholic: The Congregational Idea of the Church* (Geneva: World Alliance of Reformed Churches and Allison Park, PA: Pickwick Publications, 1986).

38 In this connection it is interesting to note that unlike those who composed the sixteenth-century Reformed confessions, those who framed the *Westminster Confession* (followed largely by the Congregational *Savoy Declaration* of 1658, the *Second London Confession* of 1677 and the 1688 confession of the Particular Baptists) introduced a chapter on adoption. Though the majority of the Westminster divines were Presbyterians, it was the Particular Baptists and the Congregationalists who drew out the implications of adoption for polity.

39 H. A. Hodges makes no bones about it. Writing of the English Reformation he declares, 'The continuation of the hierarchy, on which so much depends, was made possible by the co-operation of the Crown with the Church's leaders.' See his *Anglicanism and Orthodoxy*, 30. See Sell, *Dissenting Thought*, ch. 22; *Commemorations*, ch. 4; "Reformed identity."

40 The World Council of Churches document *Baptism, Eucharist and Ministry* (Geneva: WCC, 1982), emphasises the importance of the ministry of the whole people of God. However, relatively few churches make provision in their polity for the real participation of all members *together*. Some local churches belonging to traditions which might, historically, have been expected to do so have memberships so large that Church Meeting is a practical impossibility; elsewhere, where the excuse of numbers cannot be advanced, Church Meeting is, nevertheless, in too many cases moribund.

41 See further, Sell, *Commemorations,* ch. 14; *idem*, "By the Spirit, through the Word, within the fellowship," *Touchstone* VI (1989): 33–41.

42 For some reflections see Alan P. F. Sell, *Conservation and Exploration in Christian Theology* (Caernarfon: Gwasg Pantycelyn, 1993).

43 P. T. Forsyth, *The Church, the Gospel and Society* (London: Independent Press, 1962), 80.

44 Alan P. F. Sell, "The Reformed Family Today," 441. On re-reading my text, I note that I have referred a good deal to my own writings. This is only because

the present paper represents a distillation of themes upon which I have mused over a number of years, on some aspects of which I have been asked to write on earlier occasions.

5

THE INVISIBLE CHURCH REVISITED

Martin H. Cressey

On being invited to contribute a paper to this conference out of my experience with the Faith and Order Commission of the World Council of Churches, I looked up in the two editions of the SCM *Dictionary of Christian Theology* the articles on 'Church' and 'Ecclesiology' as a quick way of scanning some relevant topics. It was good to be thus reminded of the thoughts of Professors A. T. Hanson and J. G. Davies. It was interesting to observe that between 1969 and 1983 the separate article 'Invisible Church, Visible Church' was dropped, though the topic is still alluded to under 'Church' in the 1983 revised edition. In wondering why this should be, I was reminded of various ways in which the concept of the invisible church had played a part in my own thinking and seemed now to be acquiring new relevance. Hence my theme, "The Invisible Church Revisited."

The invisibility of the Church as a problem

I first learnt about the invisibility of the Church in the context of an evangelical Bible class. I was a teenager, bored by the services at the Presbyterian Church where my mother was a Sunday School leader. I found a niche for myself in a Sunday afternoon Bible class. After a while I began to attend an evening Bible study led by Mr. Burns, a retired civil servant, whose teaching I gratefully acknowledge as the source of a serious concern with the Bible. His was no narrow conservatism but a determination to explore the text with an enquiring mind and an openness of spirit. I particularly remember his taking us through the book of Revelation and enabling us to grasp it as a work of imagination. He himself worshipped with the Open Brethren but he did not recruit for them; he taught us that denomination was entirely secondary and that the Church was the invisible company of the faithful elect.

As an Oxford undergraduate I came under the influence of St. Columba's Church and the Presbyterian chaplaincy. Alongside my studies for Greats I began to learn about the great Reformers and to share their awareness of Augustine. The invisible church was still a theme but I was also beginning to understand the issues both of reform and of ecumenism. Later, as a candidate for the Presbyterian ministry, here at Westminster College, I was taught by a staff who were actively engaged in both those currents of church life and so was introduced to the World Alliance of Reformed Churches (WARC) and to the World Council of Churches (WCC). My pastoral ministry in a local church was in Coventry at the time of the building of the new Cathedral and of high hopes for church unity. Invited because of my evangelical antecedents to a meeting at the WCC study centre of Bossey, I recall being counselled by a senior evangelical – 'We find that those who go to Bossey are often lost to us' (note that he did not say – nor intend to say – 'lost' absolutely!). He was aware, as I had become aware, that both for Reformed theology and for the ecumenical movement generally the invisible church of the personally committed had become a problematic concept in ecclesiology.

To take seriously the ecumenical quest for visible unity and in particular organic union was to seek a structured life of the Church which did not ignore the issues which had divided denominations but rather struggled to resolve them, perceiving that these issues mattered to Christians of many traditions in a way that gave fuller meaning to the concept 'body of Christ'. The invisibility of the Church must not be expounded in ways that minimised the importance of ministry, of oversight, of councils, of sacraments. My guess is that this accounts for the change noted in my introductory paragraph between the two editions of the SCM Dictionary. So much for how I came to be involved in these issues.

I turn now to systematic treatment, beginning with the WARC and the WCC. Of all the Christian world communions that have expressed themselves in modern times through councils, conferences and commissions on the world scale, the WARC has been, in my opinion, the most careful to define its tasks in relation to the ecumenical movement as a whole. From its Reformation heritage it has drawn not only the motto *ecclesia reformata semper reformanda*, a second or third generation Reformed slogan, but also and more basically John Calvin's conviction that reform was not intentionally divisive but was directed to the cleansing and healing of the whole body of the Church. Calvin declared in a letter to Bullinger of March, 1540: 'We must needs endeavour by all the means we can, that the churches to which we faithfully minister the Word of the Lord may agree among themselves.' Later, in April 1552, he wrote to Archbishop Cranmer in England, concerning a projected conference on unity, 'I would not grudge to cross even ten seas, if need were, in such a cause.'[1] Calvin has to admit his dilatoriness in writing to Bullinger despite the urgency of the subject; he also asks whether Cranmer can find someone nearer at hand for his conference. (He was as human as we are!) In the early years of the WCC many representatives of the Reformed tradition (some thought too many!) played leading roles in the Geneva staff. Alongside the Lambeth Quadrilateral and the 1920 invitation of the Ecumenical Patriarch, Assemblies of Presbyterians and Congregationalists and Disciples made proposals that led to the calling into being of the Faith and Order movement.

Karl Barth's view as an example, with some comparisons from Orthodox ecclesiology

When the Faith and Order movement got under way, the comparative method adopted in the preparations and deliberations of the Lausanne conference did not lead to despair over the visible church but to a growing hope that visible unity and even organic union were possible and desirable. In that setting of hope the concept of the invisibility of the Church needed to be restated, notably by Karl Barth. In Chapter 62.2 of the *Church Dogmatics* IV/1, Barth emphasises that

> the Church came into being quite visibly with the calling of the twelve apostles ... It developed visibly with the addition of the thousands on the day of Pentecost ... In the world of Constantine ... it assumed visible forms ... and the Reformers ... gave themselves to the task of building on the ruins of the past a new and visible Church ...[2]

He fully acknowledges that those visible forms, Constantinian or Reformed, could be 'terrifying' but he regarded as 'ecclesiastical Docetism' the attempt at 'explaining away ... earthly and historical form as something indifferent, or angrily negating it, or treating it only as a necessary evil, in order to magnify an invisible fellowship of the Spirit and of spirits'. It is from this starting point that Barth develops his paradoxical description of the being of the Christian community as the visible object of that faith (*credo ecclesiam*) which penetrates to its invisible, spiritual reality – one, holy, catholic and apostolic.

It is helpful to read that chapter of the _Church Dogmatics_ in relation to Orthodox ecclesiology. It is often irritating to Western participants in Faith and Order drafting (a notable fairly recent case being the message of the Santiago World Conference) to meet fierce Orthodox resistance to any call for the Church to repent. It seems at first to be Christian pride and arrogance, but it is at its root not that, but a perception that it is the visible church that is the body of Christ, and is essentially as He is essentially, in his sinlessness, despite the sins of its members.

To recognise such convergence between neo-orthodoxy and Eastern Orthodoxy leads one to wonder whether the difficulties with the language of invisibility are indeed linguistic rather than substantial. The rest of this paper seeks to do two things; (a) to recall briefly the development of the invisible/visible discussion as the background to the ecumenical objections to earlier teachings about invisibility; and (b) to begin to explore certain emerging possibilities for positive use today of the concept of the invisible church.

(a) _The Origins of the Phrase 'Invisible Church' and the Visible/Invisible Contrast_

The direct uses of the terms 'invisible' and 'not seen' in the New Testament refer not to the Church but to God and his attributes and promises. God's own being and some of his attributes are _aorata_ – God's eternal power and divine nature, though understood through the things God has made and in that sense perceived, are in principle invisible (Rom 1:20). The Son of God is the visible image of God who is _aoratos_ and whose creative act in the Son includes entities which are also _aorata_ (Col 1:15–16; 1 Tim 1:17; Heb 11:27). On the other hand there are things which are not seen because they are not yet here, things which will come about through God's gracious promises; such things we hope for and await with patient conviction (Rom 8:24–25; Heb 11:1) or prepare for with foreknowledge (as Noah prepared for the flood, Heb 11:7). Both the things which are invisible in principle and those not yet seen because future are elements in God's eternal creative and redemptive purpose (2 Cor 4:18; Heb 11:3). It is because the Church is itself part of that purpose that a transference of the idea of invisibility to certain aspects of the

Church is appropriate.

In what senses can the Church as described in the New Testament be called invisible? The transference is made by considering two features of the Church as described by the New Testament writers. On the one hand the communities of Christians that emerged across the Roman Empire, communities of great diversity and with many human weaknesses, are nevertheless described by Paul as 'holy' because they belong to the holy God and are the body of Christ. There is that about them which belongs to their relation with the invisible attributes of God, Father, Son and Spirit. On the other hand these same churches move through history in struggles and interior conflicts which show up that which is false and temporary in them (including some persons outwardly members of them, cf. 1 John 2:19, who later leave the fellowship),while they also reveal that which, though not yet seen, is the promised destiny of the true faithful. This feature of the Church in history is more emphasised in the Johannine writings, but this does not lessen the importance for my theme of the Pauline understanding of the holiness of the Church. This leads me to question Professor A. T. Hanson's judgment that 'Paul believes in a Church which is visible' *in contrast with* the Johannine writings.[3] I strongly agree with Hanson in picking out from the whole of the New Testament the issue of election/predestination as the one which led to a fuller development of the concept of the invisible church.

Origen and Augustine

Thus on the one hand Origen with his concern for God's universal saving purpose, understands the Church as mystically comprising all humankind; the visible boundaries of the explicit Christian fellowship do not limit the invisible effects of God's grace.[4] On the other hand Augustine, following up tendencies both in Paul and John, had to reconcile two basic aspects of his faith: his conviction that the elect, the true members of the Church, can be known to God only; and his high regard for the sacramental functioning of the historical church. He makes the reconciliation by maintaining both the vital importance of the visible church as the normal place for finding salvation and the possibility that some are saved outside it, whereas some who are outwardly its members are not so in their hearts and so will be damned.

The Reformers

It was the Augustinian line of thought that aided Luther and Calvin in finding an ecclesiology that both gave them a continuing sense of the oneness of the whole Church of God and also enabled them to bear their separation from central structures of the visible church: '... as (the elect) are a small and despised number, concealed in an immense crowd, like a few grains of wheat buried among a heap of chaff, to God alone must be left the knowledge of his Church, of which his secret election forms the foundation'; yet at the same time, '... as it is necessary to believe the invisible Church, which is manifest to the eye of God only, so we are also enjoined to regard this [visible] Church which is so called with reference to man, and to cultivate its communion.' Small though the present number of the elect may be, now living on earth, the invisibility of the Church refers also to the fact that the Church comprises 'all the elect of God, including in the number even those who have departed this life' ... 'all the elect who have existed from the beginning of the world.'[5] Such views could also sustain the leaders of movements for more radical reformation; their enterprise aimed at a closer obvious correspondence between the visible form and life of the churches and their inward, invisible relationship with God in Christ by the Holy Spirit.

Schleiermacher

The concluding chapter of Schleiermacher's *The Christian Faith* in many ways picks up Calvin's line of thought. Barth accuses 'the great Schleiermacher' of canonising the visible church in the definition given in the heading to para. 11 of the introduction to *The Christian Faith*: 'Christianity is a monotheistic faith, belonging to the teleological type of religion, and is essentially distinguished from other such faiths by the fact that in it everything is related to the redemption accomplished by Jesus of Nazareth'.[6] 'In this definition', says Barth, 'everything has been more or less correctly perceived. The only thing is that the third dimension, in which the Church is what it is, is completely absent.'[7] Yet this stricture ignores Schleiermacher's later affirmation that, 'By the Invisible Church is commonly understood the whole body of those who are regenerate and really have a place within the state of sanctification'.[8] The Reformed understanding of the invisible/visible persists from Calvin through Schleiermacher to Barth.

The nineteenth century: evangelical, liberal and pentecostal movements

The kind of emphasis on the invisible church which I encountered as a teenager developed within nineteenth century movements which for a variety of reasons became individualistic. Pietists and Evangelicals (in the English-language sense) responding to preaching which called for personal decision found themselves both drawn together in fellowship with others of their persuasion (as in the Methodist Societies) and at the same time excluded by the traditional churches. At an opposite pole liberals sought to retain some form of personal faith while accepting critical appraisals of Bible and church history; they too placed stress on personal conviction and the fellowship of like minds and spirits. At the close of the century the beginnings of the Holiness/Pentecostal movement spoke much of the gifts of the Spirit to each true believer while realising that to follow their understanding of the Spirit's guidance they had to separate themselves (and/or were excluded) from the churches in which they had first sought and received the gifts. There were of course groups within each movement that saw themselves narrowly as the only true church, or in some cases the faithful remnant of the true church in the last days. Yet even in such groups the marks of being the true church were those of personal commitment and spiritual gifts rather than structured ministries and sacraments.

The twentieth century: WARC and WCC

I have already remarked upon the main factor that led to an emphasis in the developing ecumenical movement upon the visible church. The recovery of the New Testament view of the unity of the Church was coupled with a recognition that the churches were chiefly divided by factors in their understanding of the visible church, its members, ministry, sacraments and governance. The emergence of a truly worldwide church (an emergence which William Temple described as 'the great new fact of our era' – this rather than the ecumenical movement itself, though he is often cited to the latter effect) led on the one hand to the desire for strengthened links between churches separated by geography but one in theological tradition and church order (hence the WARC and other Christian world communions) and a conviction that parallel world bodies of a confessional type must seek reconciliation with one another. Such reconciliation required a meeting place for the churches themselves, since for the most part they did not concede decision-making authority to the Christian world communion of which they were a member. So emerged the WCC with its emphasis on the direct membership in it of churches rather than an inter-confessional federation. Traces of that tension are still apparent in the debates of the Harare WCC Assembly.

United and Uniting churches

The ecumenical concern with the visibility of the Church and with visible unity is reflected in the constitutions of the various United and Uniting churches that have come into being during the twentieth century. I use the church to which I belong, the United Reformed Church in the United Kingdom, as an example. In its Basis of Union, the fundamental text of its constitution, the URC begins from the affirmation that 'there is but one church of the one God.' There was a long discussion in the Joint Committee that drafted the Basis about how Israel is related to that concept, a debate which recalled Calvin's reference to 'all the elect that have existed from the beginning of the world.' So the first clause of the Basis continues: 'He called Israel to be his people, and in fulfillment of the purpose then begun he called the Church into being through Jesus Christ, by the power of the Holy Spirit.' This one Church is 'holy', 'catholic', or 'universal', and 'apostolic', but: 'The unity, holiness, catholicity and apostolicity of the Church have been obscured by the failure and weakness which mar the life of the Church', failure and weakness which 'have in particular been manifested in division which has made it impossible for Christians fully to know, experience and communicate the life of the one, holy, catholic, apostolic Church.' In these statements one can see the influence both of the factors that led to the development of the concept of the invisible reality of the Church despite its divisions and of the call to overcome the divisions, to manifest the Church's true nature in its visible life.

A key paragraph follows in the URC Basis. The URC 'sees its formation and growth as a part of what God is doing to make his people one, and as a united church will take, wherever possible and with all speed, further steps towards the unity of all God's people.' On the day when the URC came into being, October 5th 1972, the ceremonies were held by invitation in the Methodist Central Hall and in Westminster Abbey; Anglican, Free Church and Roman Catholic leaders joined in the commitment to seek for further steps towards the unity of all God's people. Throughout the subsequent life of the URC there has been a tension between loyalty to the aim of further union and the maintaining of Reformed principles. In the occasional gatherings of United and Uniting churches convened at their request by the Faith and Order Secretariat, similar stories have been told, which all affirm that a concept of invisible unity in Christ is not enough if Christians and those to whom they witness are 'fully to know, experience and communicate the life of the one, holy, catholic, apostolic Church.'

Summary of the case 'against'

This rapid survey thus, in my opinion, bears out the case that has been made against a certain way of understanding the invisibility of the Church. The embodiment of God's purpose requires the visibility of the human instrument through which the purpose is being forwarded, first the nation Israel and then the people who once were no people, the Church made up of those called from all nations. A balanced Reformed view recognises the invisible aspects of the Church while valuing and seeking visible unity; as Barth argued, it is the same Church that can be perceived historically and sociologically that is also the object of the faith judgment that it is the one, holy, catholic, apostolic body of Christ. From this standpoint it is understandable that ecumenical discussion has tended to avoid the description 'the invisible church,' both as misleading through its association with individualism and unnecessary in describing the Church, which is the object of both sight and faith. There are, however, it seems to me some good reasons for revisiting the invisible church not only in such an historical survey of the term but also as a concept that helps us to describe certain developing aspects of church life in the present day. To these aspects I now turn.

(b) *The Invisibility of the Church in Relation to Problems of Describing Church Renewal*

Mention has already been made of the difficulties experienced by groups within the Church that seek the renewal of its life. The sixteenth-century Reform, the radical Reformation, Pietism, the Methodist movement, the Pentecostal and charismatic movements all provide examples. The 'main line' church bodies have often rejected such groups and eventually excluded them from membership or created a situation in which the groups voluntarily (though unwillingly) separated themselves and became new 'denominations.'

Today the 'main line' churches (the phrase itself begs questions), as part of their ecumenical commitment, seek new relationships, particularly with Evangelicals and Pentecostals; they also strive to hold within their fellowship charismatic groups which could easily slip away. The Roman Catholic and Orthodox churches have had this problem more broadly, in defining their attitude to Protestants. Within the Reformed tradition conversations have been held to review the relation between 'reform' and 'radical reform,' the union of the World Presbyterian Alliance and the International Congregational Council already in 1970 involved some reappraisal of past judgments about 'reformation without tarrying for any.'

All these aspects of ecumenical outreach seem to me to require use of the concept of the invisible church. When Roman Catholics began to speak of 'separated brethren' while still holding that the Catholic Church 'subsists in' the churches in communion with the Roman magisterium; when Reformed churches stand up for the rights of members of the Society of Friends and the Salvation Army, without thereby abandoning Reformed teaching on baptism and eucharist; when the Cambridge theological federation arranges contacts with the house church movement so that ordinands may understand that movement better when they encounter it in local ministry; when the WCC struggles with questions of receiving into its membership African Independent Churches – at all such points, whether or not the words 'invisible church' are used, it is being recognised that there are manifestations of the body of Christ outside the structures which a particular Christian tradition regards as the clearly visible church.

A recent Presidential address to the Executive Committee of the World Alliance of Reformed Churches, has further emphasised the importance of this area of reflection. Dr. C. S. Song, Taiwanese Presbyterian and long-time ecumenist, challenged the ecumenical movement to realise that it has become out of touch with many Christians today who seek a spirituality more related to their daily problems than ecumenical conversations about ministry and sacraments have seemed to be. Those, like myself, who think that the conversations must still continue and do have an importance for daily Christian living, have nevertheless to find ways of speaking about contemporary spiritual and radical movements that do not undervalue their importance and relevance. To include them in the invisible church is a way of achieving this.

The invisibility of the Church in relation to encounter with other faiths

If 'separated brethren' is the pointer to one area in which the invisibility of the Church becomes once more important ecumenically, then 'anonymous Christians' is another. At the 1977 Theological Consultation on Dialogue in Community held at Chiang Mai, Thailand, a very diverse group of Christians found it possible to express their calling as Christians as follows:

> We are specifically disciples of Christ, but we refuse to limit Him to the dimensions of our human understanding. In our relationships within the many human communities we believe that we come to know Christ more fully through faith as Son of God and Saviour of the world; we grow in His service within the world; and we rejoice in the hope which He gives.[9]

This is the same spirit of outreach which led Karl Rahner to speak of 'anonymous Christians'; drawing on the hopeful view taken by the Second Vatican Council of the possible salvation of those who are not church members, Rahner wrote of the person who 'lives in a state of Christ's grace through faith, hope and love, yet who has no explicit knowledge of the fact that his life is oriented in grace-giving salvation to Jesus Christ.'[10] It has, of course, been complained that such a view is a kind of Christian imperialism, claiming as Christian every manifestation of faith, hope and love in all the world's communities of faith. Yet the approach can also be seen as Christian humility, as, for example, when I have heard Professor Lamin Sanneh speak of his Muslim upbringing in West Africa in terms reminiscent of Paul's sense of his calling from the womb within Judaism. If Reformed theology has always been able to speak of the elect within the Abrahamic tradition before the incarnation, then it is not unreasonable to speak of an election today of persons who do not yet know, perhaps never in this life know, from whom their calling has come. In conceptualising that situation the term 'invisible church' can find another extended use.

The invisibility of the Church in relation to Church/humanity issues

A third area in which the term 'invisible church' can find a new usefulness is that explored by the Faith and Order study on "The Unity of the Church and the Renewal of Human Community". In its report *Church and World*, there is an important chapter on "Kingdom-Church-Humanity" whose drafting owed a great deal to Professor Jan Lochman. A key paragraph reads:

> In the perspective of the kingdom of God it becomes possible to speak about the relation between church and world without one-sided distortion. This perspective implies, first of all, that the relation between church and world depends ultimately on a final act of God in which God's promise of redemption becomes full reality. In this way any premature amalgamation and confusion between church and world is precluded. There is, in other words, a legitimate concern for the inalienable identity of the church as distinct from the world, in the church's intrinsic relation to God the Father, Son and Holy Spirit, while at the same time the relationship between church and world is recognized and practised in hope.[11]

If, in terms of present renewal and of dialogue with people of other faiths, we may speak of an invisible present belonging to the community of grace within ambiguous relations to the visible church, the 'Church and World' theme takes us back to the New Testament passages about what is not seen because it is not yet here. To quote again:

> ... the church is called to be in all aspects oriented towards the final coming of the kingdom of which it is already a foretaste, especially in the Lord's Supper, which is the communion of Christ's eschatological meal with his people. The church anticipates the yet greater blessings which God has in store and which surpass present human experience.[12]

It is particularly significant that the Lord's Supper, which can easily come to appear exclusive, with its dismissal of even the catechumens, is here regarded as the foretaste of the most inclusive visions of God's final purpose for humankind.

The categories employed in the report itself are not those of visible/invisible but of 'mystery' and 'prophetic sign', but the treatment of these two themes aligns them with the two New Testament senses of invisibility, the invisible in principle and the invisible because not yet arrived. Thus,

> ... when the word "mystery" is applied to the church, it refers to the church as a reality which transcends its empirical, historical expression – a reality which is rooted in, and sustained and shaped by, the communion of Father, Son and Holy Spirit.[13]

Yet further:

> Called by God out of the world the church is placed in the world's service; it is destined to be God's sign for the world by proclaiming the gospel and living a life of loving service to humanity. ... If the adjective "prophetic" is attached to the term "sign", it is in order to recall the dimensions of judgment and salvation, and the eschatological perspective which inheres to the notion of mystery and is often implied in the biblical occurrences of "sign."[14]

Conclusion

In drawing together in the previous few sentences the two New Testament senses of invisibility with contemporary reflection on the church and humankind, I have been reminded of an Old Testament prophetic vision to which I have often returned in reflecting on the ecumenical movement. It is the third of the visions of Zechariah (Zech 2:1–5):

> I looked up and saw a man with a measuring line in his hand. Then I asked, 'Where are you going?' He answered me, 'To measure Jerusalem, to see what is its width and what is its length.' Then the angel who talked with me came forward, and another angel came forward to meet him, and said to him, 'Run, say to that young man: Jerusalem shall be inhabited like villages without walls, because of the multitude of people and animals in it. For I will be a wall of fire all around it, says the LORD, and I will be the glory within it.'

That picture of a city without walls that cannot be neatly measured according to its earlier dimensions and yet has a special place in God's providential action is one that I find well expressed by use of the concept of the invisible church in some of the ways I have suggested in this paper. Of course the Church is always inclined to turn in upon itself when it is in difficulties, as now in Western countries; indeed in the Revelation to John (Rev 11:1–2) there is an echo of Zechariah (and of Ezekiel's vision of the new temple) which expresses that defensive reaction to persecution:

> Then I was given a measuring rod like a staff, and I was told, 'Come and measure the temple of God and the altar and those who worship there, but do not measure the court outside the temple; leave that out, for it is given over to the nations, and they will trample over the holy city for forty-two months.'

Yet that is not the final vision of John, his vision of the city without a temple, whose light is the glory of God 'and its lamp is the Lamb. The nations will walk by its light.' (Rev 21:22–4).

My conclusion therefore is that it is worth revisiting the invisible church, to reckon with the dangers, which Karl Barth and others have pointed out, of over-spiritualizing the Church but also to estimate the refreshing power of a vision that can burst out of narrow and constricting understandings of the boundaries of the Church. I am personally very glad that the most recent (and probably the last!) opportunity I had of contributing to a major Faith and Order study was one that ended on such a note. As the Vancouver Assembly of the WCC declared in setting up the study, 'the Church can go out to the edges of society, not fearful of being distorted or confused by the world's agenda, but confident and capable of recognizing that God is already there at work.'[15]

Notes

1   Jules Bonnet, ed., *Letters of John Calvin* (Edinburgh: Thomas Constable & Co., 1855, 1857), vol. 1, 89 (with wrong date of 1539) and vol. 2, 333.

2   Karl Barth, *Church Dogmatics* IV/1 (Edinburgh: T. & T. Clark, 1956), 650 ff. (p. 653).

3   Alan Richardson, ed., *A Dictionary of Christian Theology* (London: SCM Press, 1969): "Invisible Church, Visible Church".

4   See for example *Origen: Contra Celsum* (ed. and trans. H. Chadwick; Cambridge: Cambridge University Press, 1980), IV.28.

5   John Calvin, *Institutes of the Christian Religion* (ed. J. T. McNeill; trans. F. L. Battles; London: Collins, 1975), IV.i.2; IV.i.7; IV.i.2; IV.i.7.

6   F. D. E. Schleiermacher, *The Christian Faith* (ed. H. R. Mackintosh and J. S.

Stewart; Edinburgh: T. & T. Clark, 1928), § 11, p. 52.

7   Barth, *Church Dogmatics*, IV/1, 656.

8   Schleiermacher, *The Christian Faith*, 677.

9   Stanley J. Samartha, ed., *Faith in the Midst of Faiths* (Geneva: WCC, 1977), 143.

10 Karl Rahner, *Theological Investigations* (London: Darton, Longman & Todd, 1961–84), VI, 390–98; XII, 61–78; XIV, 280–94.

11 World Council of Churches, *Church and World: The Unity of the Church and the Renewal of Human Community* (Geneva: WCC, 1990), 25.

12 *Ibid.*, 23.

13 *Ibid.*, 26.

14 *Ibid.*, 28.

15 David Gill, ed., *Gathered for Life: Official Report, VI Assembly, World Council of Churches, Vancouver, Canada, 24 July–10 August, 1983* (Geneva: WCC and Grand Rapids: Wm. B. Eerdmans, 1983), 50.

6

THE FAITHFULNESS OF 'OTHERWISE'

Walter Brueggemann

With the collapse of Christendom the Church is now in a quite changed interpretive context where new ways of knowing and speaking and living are both required and permitted; specifically *imagination* is increasingly recognised and valued as a way in which we are led and transformed by God's category-shattering, world-forming spirit. 'Imagination' may be understood as the God-given, emancipated capacity to picture (image) reality – God, world, self – in alternative ways outside conventional, commonly accepted givens.[1] Imagination is attentiveness to what is 'otherwise,' other than our taken-for-granted world.[2]

I *The refusal of 'otherwise'*

Because of the endless pressure and the insatiable need to control, it is our human wont to establish a fixed, visible, settled 'given' that is beyond criticism or re-examination, a 'given' that variously partakes of intellectual, socio-economic, political, and believing components.[3] A primary stratagem for such givenness and its defence is the refusal of any 'otherwise,' any alternative, and the rejection of the procedures whereby 'otherwise' might be made visible and/or credible.

In broad sweep one can perhaps identify the following efforts at such visible settled givenness that intends to fend off the threat of alternative:

1) The medieval system of the Church, that came to be expressed in scholastic doctrinal formulation and in sacramental administrative exclusiveness, offered a secure and certain habitat for the faithful. As it settled and developed interpretive hedges, this system became less and less open to 'otherwise,' and found convincing warrants and means to preclude imaginative acts of interpretation outside the givens.

2) That medieval system of teaching and sacrament, over a long and complicated time, came to be displaced in public perception by the 'Age of Reason,' variously 'modernity,' 'Enlightenment,' that was, among other things, a response to the shambles of the religious wars. Scientific method, coupled with autonomous reason was seen, broadly, to be safer and more reliable than the old faith that appeared to be grounded in superstition and blind tradition and was productive of bloody hostility.[4]

The logic of modernity – of which we are all children – is now, belatedly seen to be exceedingly thin and one-dimensional, giving credence to the thought and judgement of 'clear thinkers' who fenced out all emotion, who claimed they were objective and free of every vested interest, and who therefore became the voices of 'the given.'[5] This way of thinking depended upon a logic that allowed no interpretive manoeuvrability or upon clear, unambiguous experience that made things plain. This judgement was explicitly aimed, in the seventeenth century, at the Church's claims of mystery and holiness. In terms of epistemology, it resisted any practice of imagination, of alternative picturing, because rationality demanded dealing with 'the given.'[6]

There are many pointers to its spent character of that certitude. I will refer to only one. United States foreign policy, rooted in the imperial dreams of Theodore Roosevelt and Elihu Root, culminated in Franklin Roosevelt and Henry Stimpson and his several protégés who managed the American Dream into and through the Cold War. In a remarkable book, Walter Isaacson and Thomas Evan have traced the monopoly of influence on U.S. foreign policy of six men in Washington – Dean Acheson, Charles Bohlen, Averill Harrimann, George F. Kennan, Robert Lovett, and John J. McCloy.[7] What interests me is that they are termed 'the Wise Men,' the clearest thinkers who knew best and who framed and conducted U.S. foreign policy with cold, clear, rationality and utter reasonableness. The book ends, inevitably, with the sorry scene of the Lyndon Johnson White House, in which this little cadre of 'The Best and the Brightest' came repeatedly to meetings in a growing stupor, finally facing the fact that it was their 'wisdom' that led to the sorriness of Vietnam, the awareness that their empty rationality – that had become uncritical ideology – did not understand and could not understand the odd fabric of humanness that had defeated their technology.

A footnote may be added. In his pathos-filled retrospect, Robert

McNamara, a principle architect of the Vietnam effort, reflects in print on the self-deception of the entire enterprise.[8] Given the pathos of the book, however, it is not at all clear that McNamara has learned anything or has broken with the rationality of technical competence, for at the end he discerns a series of learnings to be used by the next generation of rational certitude.

In a recent television interview, McNamara re-enforced his pathos with the wistful recognition, 'We simply did not know', a mouthful indeed, deep out of the tradition of modernist certitude rooted in 'objective reason.' What was not known, and could not be known in such a given of autonomous reason, concerned the power, energy, and resilience of tradition-rooted, land-loving societies that are immune to the 'givenness' of imperial force. All of which is to say that the givenness of such reason, all over the West, when pushed to its anxious extremity, has been a given of simple, uncriticized power, inattentive to the irreducible givenness of the human. There is no need to denigrate the great good of this given, for it brought with it enormous emancipation. But when settled, unchallenged, and made into a mode of control, its emancipatory impulses have been overrun by its sheer power.

3) In this quick summary of givenness, altogether too sweeping, it is now possible, I take it, to suggest a new hegemonic given that has come abruptly behind 'The Age of Reason' that, until we see it more clearly, may be dubbed 'the Age of Information.' Its prophet is perhaps Frances Fukuyama who, since 1989 and the collapse of the Soviet Union, has gloated over the ultimate and irreversible triumph of liberal capitalism, the final elimination of any sustainable challenge to capitalism as a total, defining force in the world.[9] Of course there are deep continuities between the old claims of the Enlightenment and the new modes of capital globalisation. But they are also very different, for the Bill Gates phenomenon is not explicitly committed to the old dogmas of settled reason. Now everything is reduced to technical capacity; any question, moreover, that does not admit of surface response is sure to be a dismissed question. The difference from the older Reason may be that such simplistic technological perception is a 'dumbing-down.' Nevertheless this givenness shares with its antecedents a totalism that is intolerant of any who are not 'with the program,' including those who,

for reasons of context, have no chance to 'get with' the program. The outcome would seem to be an incredible thinning of human questions and human possibilities.

Now this rapid naming of medieval synthesis, Enlightenment rationality, and contemporary computerism is much too simplistic; and if simplistic, perhaps pretentious on my part, though I do not claim to know or understand all that is implied in this naming. My point is a simple one, that these sequenced givens are, as much as possible, totalizing, closed to newness, and resistant to criticism. Each in turn, moreover, comes to touch and shape the most elemental realities of human community and human personhood; they are therefore of primal concern to the Christian tradition with its tense, questioning relationship to every totalizing given. Such givenness characteristically thins the human spirit, makes hope lean, and saps the energy required for daring obedience.[10]

II *Making room for 'otherwise'*

The Christian tradition broadly and the Reformed tradition in particular – with its resilient impulse toward 'otherwise' – can give thanks for the fact that in recent time this interpretive tradition has important allies in the emergence of modern/post-modern hermeneutics that characteristically challenges any flat, one-dimensional notion of the given. The rise of hermeneutical awareness has permitted alternative ways of knowing that are not easily dismissed by, and that refuse to accept, the settled givens, whether they are doctrinal, rational, or technical.

1) By the 1950s, Michael Polanyi had begun to articulate an awareness that scientific learning is fundamentally a fiduciary operation that depends upon trust among researchers and therefore has an intrinsic, defining *personal* element.[11] That is, all knowledge is in some sense an interpretive act, so that we never deal simply with raw data and 'facts' that are the same regardless of the stance of the observer.[12] The introduction of the personal, interpretive, subjective element into knowledge of course undermines any thin notion of certitude – scientific, technological, or theological.

2) Polanyi's work was dramatically re-enforced in 1962 when Thomas Kuhn wrote his spectacular book, *The Structure of Scientific Revolutions*.[13] Put in over-simple fashion, it is Kuhn's argument that scientific learning does not advance incrementally by the steady accumulation of data, but by the emergence of new interpretive paradigms that drastically rearrange data. The emergence of new interpretive modes, moreover, is characteristically a *novum*, an act of brilliant hunch, of insight, of inspiration, of imagination, whereby a scholar breaks with well-established domain assumptions. The impact of Kuhn's work is inevitably controversial among scientists, but its suggestion cannot be undone. For our purposes, it is important to learn from Kuhn that knowledge is shaped – inescapably – by shrewd and compelling acts of imagination, around which data can be organised in profoundly alternative ways.

3) Closer to our own work, the contribution of Alasdair MacIntyre brings thinking like that of Polanyi and Kuhn to the work of theological adjudication.[14] MacIntyre has argued that ethical thinking is never 'objective,' that is, a flat, obvious given, but it is always embedded in a large narrative account of reality. MacIntyre proposes that we may identify three rival accounts of reality in which ethics can be embedded which he designates as Aristotle, Encyclopedia, and Genealogy. It is, moreover, obvious that embedment in any of these yields a very different ethic. It is MacIntyre's insistence that there is no ethic outside of an interpretive tradition, which in turn means that there is no thin rationality that can deliver an ethic. Every ethic requires an embedment.

4) Charles Taylor, in his exhaustive study *Sources of the Self*, has made a complementary argument that the self is never an autonomous agent, but is always an agent embedded in and generated by an interpretive tradition.[15] That is, the self is not 'given,' but is summoned in concrete context.

The contributions of Polanyi, Kuhn, MacIntyre and Taylor have the profound effect of making us aware that it could be *otherwise* than we think it to be in our dominant modes of certitude and perception. It could be otherwise, and 'otherwise' undermines and subverts every absolute claim, including those now made in thin, technical certitude that purports to float above serious commitment.

III *The burden of 'otherwise'*

It is my urging then, that imagination – the liberated capacity to picture (image) reality in alternative ways outside conventional, commonly accepted givens – is the capacity and willingness to host 'otherwise' and the actual practice of 'otherwise.' The recognition of an available 'otherwise,' whenever it is taken seriously, ought rightly to make us uneasy with our unexamined givens – even if logically secure or experientially established – because every settlement – doctrinal, national, technological – is to some extent an act of interpretation that is itself shot through with imaginative power. Even 'givens' begin in imaginative construal.

This act of imagination that inescapably constitutes our knowledge – including our scientific and our theological certitudes – acknowledges that our life in the world is not simple or flat or thin or easy or obvious; it is rather laden with interpretive potential that is not exhausted at first glance. More specifically imagination is hosted in the awareness that in, with, and under our settlements and assurances there live deep measures of ambiguity, hyperbole, incongruity, contradiction, impossibility that always break into possibility – all the powers of un-tameness that we hope to tame or keep invisible by our certitudes.

It is my insistence about this 'otherwise,' that: -

1) This 'otherwise' is the substance that has preoccupied the 'masters of suspicion' who have resisted Enlightenment thinness (Marx, Nietzsche and Freud) and the deconstructionists (Derrida, Foucault and Levinas) who understand that official certitudes in the modern West to some great extent live a lie.[16]

2) This 'otherwise' is the 'stuff' of human existence that now breaks out all around us in shrillness, the voice of the silenced now speaking, the rage of the unnoticed, the incivility of the excluded, the brutality of those who are deep into despair, but also the lyrical assertion of those driven and summoned to healed futures that stand in judgement on our present. In the face of such eruptions beyond reason, our conventional modes of control are helpless.

3) This deep 'otherwise' – note well 'deep' – is best articulated – as the

rabbis and midrashic traditions understood – in the playfulness of the biblical text that refuses thin certitude, culminating, perhaps, in the depth insights of Freud and all his derivative company.[17]

4) This forceful 'otherwise' is peculiarly entrusted to church and synagogue, ministers and rabbis, who have the most remarkable access both to the text and to human stuff, whose work depends upon thinking and speaking otherwise of a reality that cannot be acknowledged or tamed or contained by any thin certitude of doctrine, relativity, or technology. What happens in this awareness of rooted imagination is that the established reasonableness of modernity and the thin technique of post-modernity are now powerfully *de-privileged* and the totalism of technology is seen to be less than total. We are able to see that at bottom the matter of knowing is not in the givenness, for example, of rational males and rational whites against hysterical women and shrill blacks; in fact our struggle for certitude is a matter of contestation between competing acts of imagination, some of which tilt to management and some of which tilt to emancipation and the hosting of the impossible; but no *a priori* privilege is given to acts of imagination that have become established givens. While both sorts of imagination – managerial and emancipatory – are present in the Bible, the great force of the Bible, culminating in the parables of Jesus and in the impossible claim of Easter, is on the side of emancipation that 'managed care' cannot tolerate.[18]

It will be evident as I draw closer to the biblical text that I am speaking not only of competing modes of *knowledge*, but also of competing modes of *rhetoric*, because what we *say* is what we get.[19] The point is an important one and comes down, in the practice of the Church, to the enigmatic relationship between *knowledge* (reality) and *rhetoric* (speech). It is evident that where the emancipated rhetoric of the Bible occurs, it refuses to submit to old givens, but simply explodes in daring offers of a new reality that emerges in and with the very utterance. It is my judgement that much of our church rhetoric is tamed away from 'otherwise,' either by scholastic reduction or by historical criticism, to be sure that the Bible issues in nothing subversive. The struggle for faithful rhetoric in the Church is a powerful case in point of the stunning analysis of John D. O'Banion, *Reorienting Rhetoric*.[20] O'Banion organises the history of Western rhetoric into what he calls 'list' and 'story.'

'List' features among others Plato, Descartes, and the dismissal of rhetoric in the twentieth century. But these 'lists' are only intrusions into the power of 'story,' by which he means the narrative articulation of density about human life. It is O'Banion's burden to show that the 'demise of narrative' culminates in *anomie*, because human life cannot survive on or be sustained by autonomous logic that no longer embodies human 'thickness' that resists logic.[21]

IV *Enacting 'otherwise'*

I want now to consider a formidable biblical offer of the tension of settled givens and the enactment of 'otherwise,' of *list and story*, in order to show a way in which the Bible advocates and insists upon the hosting of 'otherwise'. I take as my model the books of 1 and 2 Kings. As you know, this material is essentially a fairly boring, predictable summary account of the kings of Israel and Judah that we Christians commonly label as 'history.' After Solomon, the recital is seemingly endless, about birth, capital city, mother, age, length of reign, death, place of burial, and verdict. There are, to be sure, variations dictated by particular circumstance, but these several elements account for the primary line of presentation.

What interests us now, however, is the odd intrusion into 'Kings' of the narratives of Elijah (1 Kings 17–21; 2 Kings 1–2) and Elisha (2 Kings 2–13).[22] These narratives clearly interrupt the regularised formulation of royal power and are given to us in a very different mode of expression. Moreover, they occupy about one-third of the books of Kings and in fact function not only to disrupt but also to call into question the significance of the royal account of reality. I shall urge that these prophetic narratives are indeed 'story' against 'list.' They are acts of imagination against settled, controlled certitudes, an offer of 'otherwise' in the midst of royal administration. Moreover, they are an enactment of 'otherwise' in both their historical occurrence (whatever that was) and in their canonical recurrence, inviting the on-going canonical community to host 'otherwise' in its own time and place through repeated, attentive hearing. The stories, unlike the royal list, open to the listeners in daring imagination the claim that the world does not need to be perceived or engaged according to dominant shapings of power, to privileged notions of authority, to conventional distributions of goods, or to standard definitions of what is possible.

Let me mention some obvious dimensions of 'otherwise' in the Elijah narratives:

— The prophet does not depend upon normal food supplies and will accept no junk food from the king. He is from the outset a resister (1 Kings 17:1–7). He is otherwise than a conventional character who takes royal guarantees of sustenance as a given.

— He is a source of plenty in a world defined by scarcity (1 Kings 17:8–16). He is the one who comes to the widow of Zarephath, to one fated by social power to be destitute and vulnerable, and assures her of on-going, reliable sustenance:

> For thus says the LORD the God of Israel: The jar of meal will not be emptied and the jug of oil will not fail until the day that the LORD sends rain on the earth. ... The jar of meal was not emptied, neither did the jug of oil fail, according to the word of the LORD that he spoke by Elijah. (1 Kings 17:14, 16).

Elijah is otherwise than the usual calculus of deathly scarcity in a world of royal monopoly.

— He is the source of life in a world where death is taken to be final (1 Kings 17:17–24). He does this amazing act of revitalisation – an earnest of Easter! – by prayer:

> 'O LORD my God, have you brought calamity even upon the widow with whom I am staying, by killing her son?' ... 'O LORD my God, let this child's life come into him again.' (vv. 20–21).

In his first prayer, Elijah dares to suggest that Yahweh has treated the widow like everyone else has treated her. The prayer of Elijah causes a *novum* in the life of the widow who is not privy to much newness. She must respond: 'Now I know that you are a man of God, and that the word of the LORD in your mouth is truth' (v. 24). Imagine! Life wrought for a widow in the face of death! Elijah is otherwise than all those who succumb impotently to the Last Enemy.

— He is a troubler of Israel (1 Kings 18:17). But of course this verdict is on the lips of the king. Elijah does not trouble all of Israel. He troubles royal, settled, entrenched Israel. He has not respected present power arrangements and enacts a power outside what is taken to be legitimate. His is a political act, as the king rightly perceives. But a political act is always a theological act as well. Elijah takes on the gods of Ahab and Jezebel, causes a showdown at Carmel. He defeats the prophets of Ba'al even as Yahweh defeats Ba'al. He exposes the sexual mysteries of Ba'alism as fraudulent. Elijah is otherwise than all those who get along by going along with consensus arrangements.

— He is the king's enemy (1 Kings 21:20). Everyone thought that the story of Naboth's vineyard had ended in v. 16 when Naboth was executed and Ahab secured the coveted land. But the narrator hangs around after the royal gain is established. He hangs around to see what else will happen. He warns us, Do not leave in the seventh inning! The text says 'Then' (v. 17). Then Yahweh sent Elijah. Then the story begins. It does not begin until this enactor of 'otherwise' is on stage. And then comes the threat to the royal family, an act of high treason:

> '... Because you have sold yourself to do what is evil in the sight of the Lord, I will bring disaster on you; I will consume you, and will cut off from Ahab every male, bond or free, in Israel; and I will make your house like the house of Jeroboam son of Nebat, and like the house of Baasha son of Ahijah, because you have provoked me to anger and have caused Israel to sin. Also concerning Jezebel the Lord said, "The dogs shall eat Jezebel within the bounds of Jezreel." Anyone belonging to Ahab who dies in the city the dogs shall eat; and anyone of his who dies in the open country the birds of the air shall eat.' (1 Kings 21:20–24).

There must have been a long pause upon hearing. How dare he say such things! We must honour the speech of 'otherwise' in the face of the king by a long pause every time we read it. Indeed, for ten chapters we pause, because imagination does not issue in instant reality. The speech lingers and it haunts as we wait. We wait and do not know, as communities that relish and treasure imagination characteristically wait and do not know.

There is waiting and not knowing until 2 Kings 9:36–37:

'This is the word of the LORD, which he spoke by his servant Elijah the Tishbite. "In the territory of Jezreel the dogs shall eat the flesh of Jezebel; the corpse of Jezebel shall be like dung on the field in the territory of Jezreel, so that no one can say, This is Jezebel."'

Elijah – big interruption = 'Yahweh is my El' – is a problem for the king, a hope for the poor, a dazzlement in Israel that no one could decode. The story is so improbable that it is hard to take with seriousness. Biblical critics – all of us tempted to Descartes – take the texts 'light.' They are, since Gunkel, 'legends' – not real, could not have happened, not as real as the royal lists.[23] Such reluctance on our part, however, does not intimidate or impede Elijah. He just keeps at his dangerous, God-given imagination, making all things new. He enacts 'otherwise,' showing that the world could be and would be different – concretely, decisively different.

I do not know about 'historicity,' nor does anyone else. But canonical imagination worries only a little about 'historicity.' In his parables, Jesus later said, 'It is as if ...' and we entertain the 'as if' as our true context for life.[24] I do not know about historicity. But I do know about canonicity. I know that this stuff made it into the Bible. Our fathers and mothers judged the material worth keeping, worth knowing, and worth hearing ... over and over. Whatever is 'historicity' we find ourselves addressed by this inexplicable enactor of 'otherwise,' recognising that such 'otherwise' is always inexplicable.

If this enactment of 'otherwise' made it into our sacred scriptures, we must ask, what are we supposed to hear when we hear these words? It strikes us as we listen that this imaginative material generates futures as royal lists could never do. So try this: -

When we hear a recital of Elijah, we are supposed to remember that the Christian Old Testament ends in Malachi 4:5–6 in this way:

Lo, I will send you the prophet Elijah before the great and terrible day of the LORD comes. He will turn the hearts of parents to their children and the hearts of children to their parents, so that I will not come and strike the land with a curse.

Elijah will be back. And when he comes back, he will reconcile parents and children. He will enact 'family values' so there will be no curse. He will enact what the world thinks is impossible.

When we hear a recital of Elijah, we are supposed to remember that the on-going, still living character of Elijah hovered powerfully around the life of Jesus:

— John the Baptist: '… he is Elijah who is to come. Let anyone with ears listen!' (Matt 11:14);

— Who do people say?: 'Some say … Elijah …' (Matt 16:14);

— At the mountain: 'Suddenly there appeared to them Moses and Elijah, talking with him' (Matt 17:3);

— At the cross: 'This man is calling for Elijah.'(Matt 27:47).

When the early Church pondered Jesus, cadences of Elijah rang in their ears, because they sensed that Jesus was an enactment of a dangerous, healing, liberating 'otherwise' that could not be stopped. And they remembered the earlier time when they had come face to face with 'otherwise.'

Elijah is profoundly in the midst of the story of Jesus, the old 'otherwise' in the new, embodied 'otherwise.' Jesus, no more than Elijah, is credible to the authorities. And even if the two of them are not connected in other ways, they are bound in an emerging 'otherwise' in ways that defy royal reason and call into question the entire royal arrangement.

Thus the angel announcement to Elizabeth about the son to be born, John, at the break of newness, must allude to Elijah:

> With the spirit and power of Elijah he will go before him, to turn the hearts of parents to their children, and the disobedient to the wisdom of the righteous, to make ready a people prepared for the Lord. (Luke 1:17)

Mark, moreover, surely understood, when he retold the raising of the daughter of Jairus, that he was retelling Elijah, now re-deployed by imagination to Jesus:

> When he had entered, he said to them, 'Why do you make a commotion and weep? The child is not dead but sleeping.' And they laughed at him. Then

he put them all outside, and took the child's father and mother and those who were with him, and went in where the child was. He took her by the hand and said to her, 'Talitha cum', which means, 'Little girl, get up!' And immediately the girl got up and began to walk about ... At this they were overcome with amazement. (Mark 5:39–42)

The whole collage of 'otherwise' defies the way the world is, and sets the watching, listening community into a dangerous, alternative life, an alternative not even visible as long as we stay with the settled story line of the kings. When we hear the recital of Elijah, we are supposed to name the names of the *carriers of 'otherwise'* who are closer at hand, who keep reflowing the juices of possibility. We have names in common and we each have our own inventory:

— Clarence Jordan who defied racism in Americus;

— Mother Teresa who defied poverty for the sake of life;

— Nelson Mandela who did not grow weary or cynical;

— Eugene Debs who insisted that public power must serve real people;

— Martin Luther King who dreamed beyond hate and lingers even now with power;

— Frederick Douglass and W. E. B. Dubois and Malcolm X, none of whom could make a difference, but did, and were commonly thought to be both 'Troubler' and 'Enemy.'

The phrasing conjures and makes available all these who thought otherwise and who, like Elisha in the train of Elijah, noticed the mountains covered with friendly horses and friendly chariots and friendly resources that the king could neither discern nor control (2 Kings 6:1).

When we hear the recital of Elijah, we are authorized to reconstrue our own lives out beyond the closed definitions we have too long inhaled, definitions given us by well-meaning parents, and by brutalising siblings, and by careless teachers who have flattened and boxed and caged until we are trapped in our own royal list,

— capable only of being good,

— of being angry,

— of being obedient,

— of being lustful and greedy,

— capable of only, only ...

And then comes the gift of 'otherwise' – call it Easter, call it resurrection – and we notice that on an attentive day we, like these ancients, are overcome with amazement at the gift of new life in the land of 'otherwise.' Of course all the flatteners from Ahab to Descartes to Fukuyama would not notice; and if they noticed, they would think the newness is a trick and not a newness. Elijah, however, never gives in to such cynical dismissiveness, but goes on into the land of possibility – even now.

V *The marks of 'otherwise'*

My theme is the practice of imagination entrusted to us in the Church, a capability of 'otherwise' so deep in our call, so urgent in our context, so dangerous in our practice. This practice of imagination is *textual*. It arises from the intense and sustained study of this inexhaustible text that we take as Holy Scripture. We notice regularly that this text comprises for us and offers to us what is not otherwise known. This text-driven, text-compelled imagination keeps us under the discipline of close study, for it is not free-lance fantasy.[25] The matter of the text is urgent, precisely because a 'modernist' Church – liberal and conservative – has largely given up on the text as our gospel script of 'otherwise.'

This practice of imagination is *sacramental*. Of course I refer chiefly to baptism and eucharist, for it is always 'Word and Sacrament.' We find in the grace-filled practice of water and wine and bread that these acts ripple with possibility we had been too dulled to notice; indeed people sometimes notice what we had missed in our familiarity. At the same time, I mean, beyond the two sacraments, our larger awareness that all our common practices in the community of faith are coded and loaded and freighted in density, all of life invested with holy 'otherwise,' sometimes voiced, often only signalled, giving a world well outside the royal recital; outside where visible power is operative, and food is shared, and lives are raised to newness we know not how.

This practice of imagination is *ecclesial* in its intention. That is, it intends to summon, evoke, and form an intentional community. That is, it is not romantic in terms of private address to autonomous individuals who may be uncommonly responsive, but aims to offer a community in touch with its own odd identity and its own odd purpose in the world, to live into and out of the freedom evoked in this counter-construal.

This practice of imagination is *ethical* in its passion.[26] That is, it summons those taken by its offer to a radical and enduring commitment that is articulated in concrete neighbour acts that are dangerous, done simply because we refuse to conform to dominant royal imagination.

This practice of imagination is *oppositional* in its stance, clearly offering an account of reality that is deeply contrasted with dominant imagination that is too much taken as a given. Such an oppositional stance may be enacted in many ways and need not always be one of direct confrontation. It may be nothing more than a determined refusal to accept the mandates and limits set by other acts of imagination, a resolve to proceed according to this construal of reality, without bothering to confront or refute what it opposes.

I finish with two conclusions: The first is this. I am in fact not proposing something new. I am rather naming what we do pastorally, homiletically, and liturgically in more or less haphazard ways all the time. In truth, if one examines the great hymns and prayers or sacramental cadences of the Church, it is abundantly clear that the characteristic rhetoric of the Church, when it speaks its own 'mother tongue,' is in images and metaphors and narratives and songs and oracles that make almost no concession to dominant definitions of the possible.

What is fresh in current conversation is the awareness, at the end of modernity and at the end of Christian domination, that imagination is a valued mode of knowledge, that such knowledge is not subject to the tests of dominant modes of certitude and that it may be found on the lips and in the utterances of strangely excluded, uncredentialled, seemingly irrational folk – folk not unlike Elijah.

Second, there are those who are very nervous about imagination, for it is taken (mistakenly) to be an act of autonomous fantasy in which an individual person makes claims of the sort that 'anything goes.'[27] But of course that is not what is meant in this discussion. It means, rather, to let the Bible, its words and its claims, make contact with the life-and-death issues of our own time and place, contact not originally intended in the text and contact that is not obvious or visible except by daring acts of reconstrual. Richard B. Hayes has made the point well in his recent analysis of New Testament ethics:

> I suggested above that in order to practice New Testament ethics as a normative theological discipline, we will have to formulate imaginative *analogies* between the stories told in the text and the story lived out by our community in a very different historical setting. ... the use of the New Testament in normative ethics requires *an integrative act of the imagination*, a discernment about how our lives ... might fitly answer to that narration and participate in the truth that it tells. ... *whenever we appeal to the authority of the New Testament, we are necessarily engaged in metaphor-making, placing our community's life imaginatively within the world articulated by the texts.*[28]

Such an act of imaginative construal out beyond any flat surface reading is what we do intuitively when we read scripture well and responsibly.[29] In the end it is possible to understand such an enterprise as spirit-led reading, inspired reading. That is a legitimate transposition of the point argued here, as long as we recognise the mandate of emancipated thought on the part of the interpretive community and as long as we understand that this is the work of rhetoric, the liberation to re-utter afresh what is given us in the text that refuses the sanctions of the dominant world.

Such an enterprise requires of most of the Church's interpreters a great deal of unlearning about scripture, unlearning the claims made for the casting of scripture in dogmatic formulation, unlearning about historical critical claims that serve to discount what is interpretively most demanding in the text. It is likely that our best models for such interpretation are to be found precisely in the churches of the marginal, among those not excessively schooled in modernity. Much of the Church in the West has been well schooled in resistance to 'otherwise.' The task we have and the context in which we live now require 'otherwise,' available only in the daring capacity to picture and enact afresh. It is not too late to leave an empty chair for

Elijah at Passover – or at Easter – or almost any time. Neither dogmatic certitude, historical critical flatness, nor technological thinness has been able to eliminate him from our future. If we forego his impossible presence, we are left with only the mantras of the royal list. That, of course, is not our true birthright.

Notes

1   Paul Ricoeur, of course, is the dominant source for the current discussion of imagination. See for example, "The Bible and the Imagination," in Mark I. Wallace, ed., *Figuring the Sacred: Religion, Narrative and the Imagination* (Minneapolis: Fortress Press, 1995), 144–66. Surely as important is the use of imagination by Karl Barth, on which see Timothy Gorringe, *Karl Barth: Against Hegemony* (Oxford: Oxford University Press, 1999), 268–90, especially the references on pp. 283–86.

2   By the use of the term 'otherwise,' I intend to allude to Emmanuel Levinas, *Otherwise than Being or Beyond Essence* (Boston: Martinus Nijhoff Publishers, 1981).

3   On the 'myth of the given,' see especially Mary B. Hesse in a variety of publications. See, for example, "Science and Objectivity" in John B. Thompson and David Held, eds., *Habermas: Critical Debates* (London: Macmillan, 1982), 98–115.

4   See Klaus Scholder, *The Birth of Modern Critical Theology: Origins and Problems of Biblical Criticism in the Seventeenth Century* (Philadelphia: Trinity Press International, 1990).

5   For this material, most helpful to me have been: Paul Hazard, *The European Mind: The Critical Years, 1680–1715* (New York: Fordham University Press, 1990) and Stephen Toulmin, *Cosmopolis: The Hidden Agenda of Modernity* (New York: The Free Press, 1990). See my summary statement, *Texts Under Negotiation: The Bible and Post-Modern Imagination* (Minneapolis: Fortress Press, 1993), ch. 1.

6   See Richard Kearney, *The Wake of Imagination: Toward a Post-Modern Culture* (Minneapolis: University of Minnesota Press, 1988).

7   Walter Isaacson and Thomas Evan, *The Wise Men: Six Friends and the World They Made* (New York: Simon and Schuster, 1986).

8   Robert S. McNamara and Brian Vandermark, *In Retrospect: The Tragedy and Lessons of Vietnam* (New York: Random House, 1995).

9   Francis Fukuyama, *The End of History and the Last Man* (New York: Free Press, 1995). In a subsequent book, *Trust: The Social Virtues and the Creation of Prosperity* (New York: The Free Press, 1995), Fukuyama has perhaps sought to modify his claim slightly, but not much.

10 On evangelical subversion of givenness, see Timothy Gorringe, *Karl Barth: Against Hegemony*. Gorringe's discussion concerns Barth's stance regarding political hegemony. He does not extend the question to include intellectual or theological or economic moral hegemony, though the point is deeply implicit in Barth's perspective. It does happen that the 'Barthian tradition' itself is on occasion tempted to its own version of hegemonic domination.

11 Michael Polanyi, *Personal Knowledge: Towards a Post-Critical Philosophy* (Chicago: University of Chicago Press, 1958). For an acute theological reflection on the work of Polanyi see Lesslie Newbigin, *Proper Confidence: Faith, Doubt, and Certainty in Christian Discipleship* (Grand Rapids: Eerdmans, 1995).

12 On the split of 'fact' and 'value' see Lesslie Newbigin, *Foolishness to the Greeks: The Gospel and Western Culture* (Grand Rapids: Eerdmans, 1986).

13 Thomas Kuhn, *The Structure of Scientific Revolutions* (Chicago: University of Chicago Press, 1962).

14 Alasdair MacIntyre, *Three Rival Versions of Moral Enquiry: Encyclopedia, Genealogy, and Tradition* (Notre Dame: University of Notre Dame Press, 1990), and *Whose Justice? Which Rationality?* (Notre Dame: University of Notre Dame Press, 1989).

15 Charles Taylor, *Sources of the Self: The Making of the Modern Identity* (Cambridge University Press, 1989).

16 On the 'masters of suspicion,' see Paul Ricoeur, *Freud and Philosophy: An Essay on Interpretation* (New Haven: Yale University Press, 1970). The work of Derrida, Foucault, and Levinas in quite different ways are congruent with Ricoeur's program of suspicion.

17 See Geoffrey H. Hartman and Sanford Budick, eds., *Midrash and Literature* (New Haven: Yale University Press, 1986), and Susan A. Handelman, *The Slayers of Moses: The Emergence of Rabbinic Interpretation in Modern Literary Theory* (Albany: SUNY Press, 1983).

18 With specific reference to the parables as 'limit expressions,' see Paul Ricoeur "Biblical Hermeneutics," *Semeia* 4 (1975): 107–45.

19 On the relation of *say* and *get,* see Walter Brueggemann, *Theology of the Old Testament: Testimony, Dispute, Advocacy* (Minneapolis: Fortress Press, 1997), 117–44. It is impossible to overestimate the decisive importance of the exact articulation of Israel for the God who is 'given and gotten' in the text of the Old Testament.

20 John D. O'Banion, *Reorienting Rhetoric: The Dialectic of List and Story* (Pennsylvania: Pennsylvania State University Press, 1992).

21 *Ibid.*, 108.
22 Along with Elijah and Elisha, attention should be paid to Micah (1 Kings 22), perhaps the most generative of any of these prophetic narratives. I have, however, limited my attention to Elijah for practical reasons.
23 On the history of critical scholarship – with particular reference to Hermann Gunkel – and its residue of problems, see Rick D. Moore, *God Saves! Lessons from the Elisha Stories*, JSOT Supp. 95 (Sheffield: JSOT Press, 1990).
24 While 'as if' seems a correct rendering of the way the parables are presented, I might prefer simply 'as' that concedes nothing about 'reality.' On the 'copula of imagination,' see Garrett Green, *Imagining God: Theology and the Religious Imagination* (San Francisco: Harper and Row, 1989), 73 and *passim*.
25 J. R. R. Tolkien, "Tree and Leaf," in *The Tolkien Reader* (New York: Ballantine Books, 1966), 68–75 and *passim* offers a nice distinction between fantasy and imagination.
26 Above all, it has been Richard Kearney who has insisted upon and explored the ways in which imagination is an ethical undertaking. See *Wake of Imagination* (St. Paul: University of Minnesota Press, 1987), *Poetics of Imagining* (London: Routledge, 1991), and *Poetics of Modernity: Toward a Hermeneutic Imagination* (Atlantic Highlands: Humanities Press, 1995). In the latter, see his discussions of Levinas, Derrida, and especially Jan Patocka.
27 So careful a critical exegete as Bernhard Anderson has seen that imagination permits freedom under the discipline of the text, and is not indiscriminate fantasy. Anderson, *Contours of Old Testament Theology* (Minneapolis: Fortress Press, 1999), 36, writes: 'But the symbolic power of the language transcends the social location and the historical circumstances in which it was originally expressed and was released with new power when the tradition became *scripture* for the community of faith. The task of the biblical theologian is to enter and understand the biblical world(s) construed by imagination. When the symbolism finds an echo in our poetic response, as "deep calls to deep" (cf. Ps 42:7), the Bible may speak today with the power of the world of God.'
28 Richard B. Hays, *The Moral Vision of the New Testament: Community, Cross, New Creation: A Contemporary Introduction to New Testament Ethics* (San Francisco: Harper, 1996), 298–99.
29 For a powerful model of such imaginative construal, see Ellen F. Davis, *Imagination Shaped: Old Testament Preaching in the Anglican Tradition* (Valley Forge: Trinity Press International, 1995).

7

THE IMPORTANCE OF COMMUNITY IN THE LONELINESS OF MODERN TIMES:
A Challenge to Reformed Theology

Eberhard Busch

I *The nature of the Christian community in the early Reformed period*

If we want to know what is the gift and the task of Reformed people for today and tomorrow, we have to know, too, what it means to be 'Reformed.' As such we cannot look forward without first looking backwards to the beginnings of the Reformed churches: not to preserve a holy tradition, much less to conjure up the 'heritage of the Fathers' in some sort of fear about the survival of a special church. If we think in this way, we have to hear again the words of Jesus: 'Whoever will save his life shall lose it; and whoever will lose his life for my sake shall find it' (Matt 16:25). But the point is to take seriously the fact that Reformed church history does not begin with us, that we rest on the shoulders of our predecessors. And thus it is valid also in relation to our spiritual parents to recall what the Heidelberg Catechism has to say of the fifth commandment,

> ... that I have to pay to them all honour, love and loyalty and to accept all good doctrine and criticism with proper obedience and to be patient with their defects and mistakes, because God wants to rule us by their hand.[1]

We have no future except one which is bound together with those who have gone before and from whom we descend, believing that God is not a God of the dead, but of the living (Luke 20:38) and that they all continue to live in him, and therefore they have the right to join in our thoughts and decisions. In this sense I ask, how they might explain to us what is meant by the notion 'the Church of Jesus Christ.' Their fundamental answer is given in that they understand the meaning of Church, more than is the case in Lutheran or Roman Catholic theology, as lying very close to the literal sense of *ekklesia*: as assembly; therefore they see the archetype of the Church in the concretely assembled community. There are three significant points I wish to make in relation to this.

I.i The decisive point is: the Church lives completely on the will of its Head, who by his free grace makes men and women belong to him. *He* assembles them and this makes them *His* community and not simply a community that emerges out of the decision of its members to assemble themselves. It emerges from that and it continues in that, that *He* is their Head, who calls them out of humankind and transplants them out of their natural surroundings into a new context, created by *Him*, in which they are connected with *Him* and with others. This context has its reason and its existence by *Him*, who makes *Himself* their head and them *His* body: by *His* effective and active word; by *His* consolation and *His* claim to them; by *His* distinct affection and faithfulness with regard to them. Thus the Theses of Berne in 1528:

> The holy, Christian Church, of which the head is Christ alone, is born out of the word of God. The Church remains in it and does not listen to the voice of a stranger.[2]

Or the Heidelberg Catechism:

> The Church is that which the Son of God gathers, protects and keeps, a congregation of those, whom He by His spirit and by His word elects and calls out of the entire human race in order to give them eternal life.[3]

There are two exclusions that are included in this concept of the Church. *On the one hand*, there is opposition to a concept of the Church which is constituted simply by the gathering and joining together of its members. In that case it is not born out of the Word of God, but out of the sociable urge of kindred spirits. The difference between both concepts is not that the members are assembled in a voluntary way here and in a forced way there. The difference is that the freedom of assembly is justified in another way here and there: here with the natural ability to choose the membership in a club which seems desirable and suitable to us; and there with the grace, which happens to us and calls us into the community of Jesus. And the difference then becomes manifest in that in a community born out of the sociable urge of kindred spirits there develops a society of equals, in fact a society that is about the exclusion of unequals, in the sense of the exclusion of those who do who do not fit in their circle, whereas the Church as gathered by the call of God must be open to being an assembly of unequals.

On the other hand, the understanding of the constitution of the Church only by its Head implies a rejection of an hierarchical concept of the Church – because Jesus Christ is the one office-bearer of his community, who gathers, protects and keeps it. Since he provides this Himself by His spirit and His word, He cannot and need not be replaced by an earthly substitute. This excludes any idea of the dominance of an active church hierarchy over against a passive laity, whether it is justified through the hierarchy's role as a mediator of salvation, or through its competence to satisfy people's religious consumerist demands and wants. Certainly, there is in the community, under the Headship of Christ, a human administration, too. But this is a function *within* the community, not above it; it is not head in and of itself, but a service in the body of the one Head which is Christ. It is a good idea that not only the ecclesial administration, but at the same time every Church member participates in the same way in Christ's triple office. They all take responsibility in their own fashion and with their talents, which is not delegated to an office above them, as little as a supra-regional church government above the communities may be more than a confederation of the communities and therefore it must not incapacitate them. Certainly on the one hand the Church is an assembly of dis-equivalence, diversity and difference, but on the other hand at the same time all members are equal in this respect that they are brothers and sisters in Christ.

I.ii Since Christ alone is the head of the community, all others in it are only members of His body, certainly entrusted with different *charisms*, but in this way, that all are simply brothers and sisters. It is a strange thing, that their head is called 'the Son of God'. This title reminds us of the fact that, 'we are accepted by grace as children of God for the sake of Christ'.[4] Here we see the profundity that the Heidelberg Catechism (4.5) does not judge the sin only formally as non-fulfilment of a demand; the Catechism sees God's law, taught by Christ, in content filled by the double commandment of love.

Therefore sin is the reversal of our relation to God and at the same time to our fellow human beings. Therefore redemption in Christ has its significance at the same time in this vertical and horizontal relation, which are to be distinguished, but not to be separated. By making human beings children of God on account of His grace, the Son of God makes them brothers and sisters one with another. By joining Himself together with them and them with God, He joins them together at the human level too, by abolishing their separation and distance, but not by levelling their difference, so that difference no longer means contrast, but instead is a 'reconciled difference.' In this sense the old Reformed interpreted the *'sanctorum communio.'* Thus Calvin:

> If we truly are convinced, that God is the Father of all and Christ the common head, then there is no choice, being united in brotherly love they cannot but share their benefits with one another.[5]

Thus a Lasco's catechism:

> As the true members of Christ's congregation together have community with their head and with all His benefits, so they have all gifts common by love for edification.[6]

Thus the Heidelberg Catechism:

> All believers have as members, community at Christ the Lord and at all His treasures and gifts; therefore each is to make use of his or her gifts willingly and with joy to the well-being and salvation of the other.[7]

Thus the Westminster Confession:

> All saints, that are united to Jesus Christ their Head, by His Spirit, and by faith, have fellowship with Him in His grace, sufferings, death, resurrection, and glory: and, being united to one another in love, they have communion in each other's gifts and graces, and are obliged to the performance of such duties, public and private, as do conduce to their mutual good, both in the inward and outward man.[8]

Certainly, this understanding of the Church includes ethics, a spiritual one and a social one. It belongs to the ethics of spirituality that according to its being assembled and being edified by its Head, the congregation has the task to assemble and to edify itself, whereas social ethics, according to the confessions (see Westminster above), is crucial to the connection and community of different human beings, which is given by Christ and which is practised in mutual love.

But it is important to understand that the social dimension is not only a matter of ethical consequences which we have to draw out of the work of God done for us. By the love of God for us we are put into a situation which we have to confirm by our doing, but which is not to created by us, because it is already created by God; certainly, we can sin against it, but we can not abolish it. In God's love both dimensions are joined together: the vertical and the horizontal, so that they belong together indissolubly. Therefore we cannot live in spiritual community with God, except we live in the social community with our fellow human beings, given to us by God.

I.iii This understanding of the Church, developed from the notion 'assembly', means that it is a dynamic, not a static matter. The Church is in motion, it is in movement in a double direction. The Church lives in a temporal movement and this is why the concrete assemblies, which are the archetype of the Church, have to take place again and again. And, this is why, while doing this, according to the practice of the Reformed tradition, preaching does not follow the revolving cycle of *pericopes*, but takes place through a *lectio continua* along the course of the books of Scripture. Furthermore, that this community in its psalmody sees itself on the way with God's people Israel, all this points to the *temporal* movement in which the Church exists. This indicates its provisional nature, in which it approaches to that which is more than the Church – the kingdom of God. 'After having accepted the gospel of God's free gracious love, we wait, until God evidently will reveal what now still is hidden in the hope'.[9] The Church exists in pilgrimage, suffering, struggling, sighing:

Destroy the works of all evil power, which rises against you, and all machinations against your holy Word, until the completion of your kingdom will come, in which you will be all in all.[10]

And at the same time, in its pilgrimage the Church has to be open to the ever

new challenges for confessing its faith and to respond to the ever present
new promptings of the Holy Spirit, who will lead us into all truth (John
16:13). All the while examining its life for what corresponds to the will
of God here and now and for what contradicts God's will for his Church.
That points already to the *local* movement, in which the Church exists
too: the missional-diaconal sending of the assembled community into the
surrounding society. Since here the community does not live primarily in
the opposition of a hierarchical office to the laity, but as the body in which
all members are gifted with *charisms*, it is prepared to perceive the *raison
d'être* of the Christian community in relation to the larger society as being
found in the execution of its sending into this society. In the Communion the
deacon's office receives his task to visit the sick people and injured persons.
There is after Calvin also a general Deacon's office of all laymen. And since
the Church is determined by its ministry of service and witness, the direction
is also clear in which its sending has to proceed. According to Calvin it is
rooted in the common meal of the Eucharist, by which it is impressed on all
participants:

> We can not hurt, nor despise, nor repudiate, nor disparage, nor somehow
> offend one of our brothers or sisters, without to hurt, to repudiate, to offend
> at the same time in them Christ ... We cannot love Christ, without loving
> Him in our brothers and sisters ... And as no part of our body suffers pain,
> which does not let suffer the whole body at the same time, so it is impossible
> to bear that one of our brothers or sisters is struck down by an evil, when
> we do not suffer from it together with them ... Because nothing can incite us
> more to mutual love than the fact that Christ gave himself to us; by this he
> asks us to dedicate and to give ourselves to one another.[11]

II *The problem of human loneliness in modern times*

What I call to mind of the understanding of community from the earliest
period of Reformed theology looks like an alien element as soon as we
consider the human situation at the end of our century. It is of course not
inevitably made redundant or anachronistic by this consideration. But if we
compare the old Reformed understanding of community and that which see
in present times, there is still a greater difference of understanding than
simply that which would emerge as the natural result of a temporal distance
of almost five hundred years. After all, the theological perspective of the

Reformed view can help to make visible the peculiarity and the problem of the modern human situation. It goes without saying that I can paint only a rough outline of it, namely through giving a Western European view, though even then, not everyone in my regional context of the world would necessarily hold to the same view. Nevertheless, maybe there are, in some of what follows, points which might have more global implications. I characterize the contemporary situation with the key word *'loneliness.'* This includes, but only in a secondary sense, experiences of 'forlornness' or 'desolation.' Neither, do I intend to mean by this those useful times of seclusion, which we need like the inhalation besides the exhalation. What is meant, on the contrary, is to find this phenomenon of 'loneliness' even in the midst of a bustling busy life. For what I intend to mean with this term at is that categorical self-understanding of the human person as being determined only through his/her self-centred individuality. This self-understanding is not simply to be condemned as egoism in a moral sense, for it need not necessarily show like that. But it lives by a definition of humanity in which relationships to fellow human beings are not to be considered essential. The human being as such counts here as a nature, which is an entity existing for and by itself, which in the innermost part, where it is completely itself, is unrelated and alone with itself. This I call its *'loneliness.'* Certainly it will also have contacts with the world outside. But it will understand the beings outside of itself as solitary individuals analogous to its own individuality, so that it can conclude from it to them, so that in them it recognizes itself, so that those contacts affirm its starting point with the definition of humanity by its isolated individuality. *Cogito ergo sum*, this Cartesian sentence stands at the beginnings of modern times.[12] 'I am' – this is the first principle fixed by myself, the highest certainty, from which I come in all my thinking and doing and to which I will always return, of which I believe that I may and must trust on it, what above all calls on me, what wants to develop in all directions, what by all the following only can be affirmed, but not limited. Friedrich Nietzsche, the prophet of this humanity, interprets that sentence like this: 'I am in "azure solitude."'[13] This anthropology of the solitary human has consequences.

II.i Humanity as determined through the prism of the isolated 'I am,' without being founded, destined and limited by the over-againstness and yet also the togetherness of the Other, sets up a world, in which this 'I-individual' would like to extend itself unlimitedly. What it discovers outside of itself, is the 'Not-I', as Johann Gottlieb Fichte said it, that is: not limitation, but material, in order to dominate or to annex it by appropriation, raw material, which is available to the grasping of the self-centred individual, which is worthless in itself, but which by that grasping, by this, what I produce with it, becomes valuable, which is transformed because of that, namely into private property of this individual.[14] Already the preacher of the principle 'I am' said, that the implications of it are that thanks to it we can make us 'dominators and owners of nature'.[15] Another consequence of this principle is that by making the material useful this individual not only gets rich, but makes himself/ herself valuable all the more – and he/she is forced to do it – in order to make himself/herself not worthless. This leads to an attitude which is indicated by Viviane Forrester: you have 'to earn to live, in order to have the right to live.'[16] And this leads to a compulsion to produce, which is so obsessive – as it is taught by Günter Anders[17] – that more is produced, than is needed, that one begins to make products, not because they are needed, therefore it is necessary to produce with them the feeling that you need them; and finally there is such an abundance that certain groups of people become superfluous. What the self-expanding individual discovers outside of it are not only things, but on the other hand also other self-centred individualistic beings, who in a similar way do expand themselves, who also are engaged in such grasping. There is conflict in the air; because co-existence is excluded here. There is no choice but to live in rivalry with others. This does not have the good or benign sense of a cheerful competition. For it means, in a secret or open way, to be at war with others. Because one pursues his or her advantage, he or she is forced to accept the disadvantage of the other and actually even to wish it. While wanting to have more than *before* for his/her own, it does mean, too, that s/he wants to have more than the *other*, and in order to avoid open war, this human will be concerned to find moral or legal or political means and tools which will make others be content with less. Karl Barth said: 'The solitary human being is the potential and in some fine or rough form also the actual *enemy* of all others.'[18]

II.ii In this anthropology of the solitary human being, the isolated 'I' has not only no others as real and true opposing individuals in order to co-exist with, but paradoxically finds that it no longer has 'itself' there either, but looses itself too. It is not right, as we have been told since the Enlightenment, that the human being, understood as just such an individual, is at least a free creature, which then afterwards can add to its freedom some social relations. Free is exactly what this human being is not! For freedom is not his fictitious potency to be able to do everything. A being is free that is able to limit itself, in order to want and to do a specific thing. But the isolated individual 'I' of Enlightenment thought cannot limit itself, since in its definition of humanity coexistence with others is not put in the first place. And if it is not free, it is not strong as well, even though it is suspiciously eager to present itself as being strong on the surface. Its aggressiveness expresses the inner weakness of its alleged primacy. That is why this isolated individual has to try to fill itself by its grip on the outside, because it is empty in itself. The isolated humanity, in itself thought as having no relationships; the definition of being a human by the mere sentence 'I am' is the description of a lonely, meaningless emptiness. And this is why the human who defines itself in this way does not realize that it, by trying to make as much as possible dependent on it, in fact becomes dependent itself, a pawn, moved around from here to there. This way it loses exactly that which it wants to defend convulsively: its self-determined and self-affirmed personality. The lonely becomes a mass human, part of a diffuse crowd, a driven and driving wheel in a big machine, led now by an authoritarian *Führer*, now by an opaque collectivism, now by anonymous powerbrokers – an element of the 'mass,' in which the names become indifferent and the different humans interchangeable and replaceable figures, in which you can disappear unnoticed: you with your particular story of your life, with your conscience and with your convictions and finally with your physical existence. Ortega y Gasset has described this modern phenomenon of the 'mass', and he wanted to fight against it by invocation of the elitist individual. But here he has ignored that the modern phenomenon of the 'mass' is itself the fruit of modern individualism, the fruit of defining humanity by a being, which in its unrelated, empty individuality counts as human. But Ortega is right to say that this 'mass' human believes itself, 'to be alone in the world'.[19] Indeed, this human is alone in the direct sense of the word, and is in danger of suffering from depression, from feelings of 'forlornness' and desolation. Because the 'mass' is a substitute for true coexistence with others, which is closed for those, who want do be defined by their mere individuality. In the 'mass' human beings do not live *together*, but live nothing but solitary individual lives unconnected *side by side*. To live this way, *side by side*, gives rise to an unlinked coexistence which produces life as a foreign exchange. 'Nothing longer-term' is the motto that Richard Sennett has used to describe the culture of this 'New Capitalism', and insightfully he remarks of a life lived by this motto: while it looses 'the bonds of confidence and commitment', it undermines at the same time 'the most important elements of *self-respect*'.[20]

II.iii The anthropology of the solitary human being has the result that we can only confer humanity on others, strictly speaking, on condition that their 'otherness' is faded out and that they are similar to or rather equal with us. Since the Enlightenment this thought has proved so fascinating, because it could mean a great liberation, namely that 'without respect of person' all human beings were to be acknowledged as having equal rights. This is a truth never to be abandoned. But the selfsame thought has caused other consequences also, in which it was not able to say what it wished to say. By way of illustration: if love is given on condition that the human being next to me has to be equal with me or similar to me, then my love is a modification of self-love, in which in fact I recognise myself in the other and insofar as I love then myself, and insofar as this love has something to do with the human being next to me, the other's value is measured by a criterion, in which I define what is and is not suitable for me. Thus the 'otherness' of the other is removed in the event of love. The thought of equality, which is removed by the solitary individual and which must fade out the 'otherness' of the other, this thought developed in different directions, but belonging together.

On the one hand in the direction of the deliberate attempt to level all human beings with one another, supported by manipulations, in order to adjust them to each other. A dubious fruit of that anthropology was the Nazi slogan of the enforced conformity (*Gleichschaltung*) of all humans and their groups to the unity of the one *Volk*, proclaimed in order to make everybody obedient without contradiction and discrepancy. The present hegemony of the various forms of mass media also causes such an adjustment and in far more subtle ways, but with equally seductive possibilities, because certainly they don't say to us *what* we have to think, but *about what* **we have** to think: and by their, 'agenda-setting' they predestine indirectly, but deeply, what we have to feel as important or what we may forget. According to Paul Virilio, we have to notice the still greater danger in the grave process that the encounter with real human beings today is beginning to be replaced by the digital and virtual appearance of figures which nevertheless look and sound human.[21] And at the close of the last century the anthropology of the solitary human achieved its climax in the realisable plan to produce humans which are genetically identical with themselves.

On the other hand, there is an even more dangerous consequence of that humanity, in which the individuals are counted as human, insofar as they are equal to or the same as each other. This understanding of humanity reveals its inhumanity in its reverse: that the unequal – those who are not to be integrated into the group defined by equivalence and sameness, the 'others', the 'strangers' – they then are to be counted as inferior, as superfluous, as useless boarders, as worthless to live, as class enemy, as race enemy, as public enemy. We know that by far it was not only the evil of the Nazi government that meant that equalization construed as enforced conformity would mean the elimination of a multitude of unequals/selection/apartheid. It seems that the self-centred individuality strictly *needs* the denial of those who are deemed unequal in order to establish a society of equals. Peter Singer has asked: 'How are we to live?' – namely on condition that the isolated individual only pursues its own interest and that of its equals; how then others can have an ethical meaning for us? He answers that we should consider that others are also individuals like us, who pursue their own interests. Singer himself is so little satisfied by his answer that he believes that humans will not be persuaded to do it (that is, to consider others) by such so-called 'rational arguments'.[22] The mistake is that he wants to heal the evil with means which are its origin. The condition of his thesis itself must be called into question, in order to get rid of the evil.

III *The challenge for Reformed theology*

Let us remember in light of this of this situation the dictum of Gustavo Gutierrez, that the origin of his liberation theology was the insight: 'The acknowledgment of the other is a still unsettled question'.[23] This raises the urgent task, of which the sociologist Sennett has said that it rather belongs to religious ethics than to political economy: that task, in which it is necessary to stem against the situation we have been describing by the integration of human beings into a 'We,' which, according to him arises where it becomes clear that there is 'No community, as long as the differences are not acknowledged in it'.[24] Similarly, the philosopher Jürgen Habermas defines this task as the work for a human society founded on the principle: 'The equal

position [of the humans in it] is that of unequals, who nevertheless know
their togetherness.'[25] But he thinks that this task today can only fulfilled
'without religious support'.[26] If this means that Christian theology failed in
this task to such an extent that people cannot wait for theological help in
this matter, then theology has to consider that criticism repentantly, and it
will be grateful to them, who are engaged in this task without such support,
and will be grateful by recognizing that theology is needed in the same
task. But if the renouncement of theological support in that task means that
such possibilities as we have been considering for communal life are to be
achieved today principally only by the abandonment of God, then Reformed
theology can not submit to that, because – even if it is acknowledged only
from the side of theology – the reference to God is not a side issue or
irrelevant matter, which can be disregarded, because you can come to the
same result without it. According to theology's insight what is at stake here is
the last reason by which the anthropology of the solitary human is called into
question as it is overcome by the anthropology of the co-existence of diverse
individuals. After all, Habermas has difficulty in giving reasons for the equal
position of those who are unequal without such support, and he does it in a
nearly tautological way, by deriving the equality of the humans from their
personality and their inequality from their individuality.[27] To me, this seems
to be too dark and reminds us of two things: if Reformed theology has not
to be ashamed of the company of such secular thinkers, it has more reason
to be not ashamed of the gospel; *and* if Reformed theology has failed in that
task and if it has itself supported in its younger history an anthropology of
the solitary human, it still has a capacity in the notion of community it finds
in the origins of Reformed theology, which is a theological orientation that
can be fruitful in considering the modern human situation. Once more I give
three indications.

III.i It is a task of the most urgent priority – not only for the Reformed, but
for them as well as for others, to confront the *anthropology* of the solitary
human with the *theology* of the not-solitary God, who is the 'Other' because
He lives in love. Let us remember the unusual formulation of the former
Reformed, that all members of the community have 'community *at* Christ
the Lord'. This means, that for them the creative centre in order to be a
community is He, in whom God commits Himself to in the decision to be
and to live in community with them. This also indicates the important

meaning of the worship in the church service in which this communicative God is to be proclaimed, invoked, praised and celebrated. This also points to the fact that the notion of a 'community of difference' is not a general idea for Christians, which could be separated from or could be applied only afterwards to that which is witnessed in the church service, but it has its solid and innovative foundations in the lively reality, in which God connects Himself with humans who are different from Him, in which therefore the anthropology of the solitary human is discovered as mischief and is denied in its origin. Speaking of the not-solitary God, Reformed theology today, more thoroughly perhaps than did the Reformed theologians of a previous age, has to put an end to the mistaken Western understanding of monotheism, understood as the identification of an absolute One, of a completely unrelated highest being, existing only for itself, with the God as witnessed to in Scripture. Without difficulty we can recognize this deity, which in fact is absolutely lonely, as the source and as the mirror reflection of that individual, which stands by itself alone. This God is an idol beside the God, who is the One only in His love, who as such is really not alone. But the wrong type of monotheism is only removed, if it is clear, too, that God is *not* dependent on human beings who have to redeem (as it were) a solitary God from his loneliness. According to the gospel it is God alone who frees human beings from their loneliness. And God can do it, because already in the roots of His being He is not alone. That is the sense of the doctrine of the Trinity – that God in His eternal life already denies loneliness, because He is in Himself real love. And that is the sense of the doctrine of creation, that just this God is able and willing, to allow and to give, beyond the triune nature, existence to beings, who are not the same like Him, but different from Him, in order to be together with them, in order to love them and to be loved by them. And these beings, who as God's creatures are different from the Creator, do exist as far as they are concerned in difference and diversity, in order to co-exist in this variety. This being in difference in relation to God and to other creatures therefore is not a mistake, which is to be removed; it belongs to the good creation, which is affirmed by God. 'It is not good, that the human being is alone' (Gen. 2:18); it is good that it is not alone. Evil is that through which sin comes into the world; in the fact of sin humankind denies both their being in difference as created by God, and the destination of the different to mutual co-existence. It is evil because of the misery that humankind becomes solitary in this way. But that is the sense of the doctrine of redemption, that in the lonely crucified one of Golgotha, God takes care of that human loneliness, takes it upon Himself and overcomes it this way, in order to open a glorious future to the separated: 'And God will dwell in them, and they will be His people' (Rev 21:3). To pass on the message of this not-solitary God, that is the first task of the Reformed theology in the human situation of today.

III.ii Only now is theology able to contradict thoroughly the anthropology of the solitary human in its own field. Let us remember the insights of the earliest Reformed thinkers that by God's love to us, who are different from Him, is given us a life in two dimensions: the relation to God and to our fellow human beings, in and with our being children of God we are to be brothers and sisters to each other. Both belong together inseparably. If with regard to God humans cannot be lonely, because God has connected Himself with them, then we also cannot be lonely on the human level, because God in Christ has connected Himself solely with me alone. In this knowledge is a wisdom, which today, more than was done by previous Reformed theologians, is able to extend our understanding of humanity. We replace that definition derived from a wrong conception of a solitary monotheism, as well as the dubious anthropological monism which we have been describing: that definition of humanity, in which the 'other,' the fellow human being is not to be found, but is excluded. This definition is to be replaced by the other, richer, definition of humanity, in which co-existence with diverse and different fellow human beings is seen as essential and fundamental to being human, not simply an enforced conformity with equals or with those who are similar to us, but with real others. Let us remember, according to biblical thinking, that it is precisely the excluded, the undesired, the strangers, the imprisoned, the hungry that are the representative sentinels of humanity. So that, if we deny our togetherness with such others, then God can no longer be God for us; so that then we ourselves are no longer human, but inhuman. Karl Barth said: 'Inhumanity is each supposed humanity, which is not already in its root and from its beginnings humanity in togetherness [*Mitmenschlichkeit*]'.[28] The anthropology of the solitary human is the doctrine of the inhuman. If humanity at its roots is humanity in togetherness, then the solitary inhuman cannot become human through building up first a strong individuality for themselves and then additionally try to develop relations to others. It is precisely the other way round, only in relation to others is my sense of self given, received and strengthened. Only in relation to the 'other' can they become that which without others they can only desire in vain: that is to be a person who stands on its own legs and thinks with its own brain. On the tracks of these thoughts runs the I-Thou-personalism of Martin Buber. The weakness of his attempt is not that he restricts humanity to the mere relation of two individuals, because he rightly is interested to say that humanity is the togetherness of different. The weakness lies in his idea that other human beings become my neighbours, the Thou by the attitude, which I have to take in relation to them.[29] There the starting point is the isolated I, which makes others to fellow creatures. And there the togetherness with them is merely an ethical duty, something which has no reality except if it is realized by me. Instead, we have to insist that humanity in togetherness is not merely a possibility, which is only to be realized by our work, or which we arbitrarily may choose for us or not, but it is a reality which is given in and with the relation between God and us. Only this way it is clear that a human being in its life without the others contradicts not only God, but at the same time itself. It is not only disobedient to God's law, but is at the same time inhuman.

III.iii However, this reality, created and given by God, includes a certain ethical task. Let us remember that for earlier Reformed theologians there was no question but to understand the practice of the inter-human community as an event of mutual love, of being loved and of loving. In this connection all depends on the mutuality. This has to do with the fact that such a love is not only gentleness, but that in it mercy and justice inseparably belong together. This also explains in which sense an everyday word in the midst of the ethics of the Kingdom of God in the Sermon on the Mount could become truly the Golden Rule, so that it no longer means the uninspired '*do ut des*', which can be integrated in the anthropology of the solitary human too, but the very new: in the name of Jesus Christ I am allowed to expect, that the others will be brothers and sisters in relation to me, and I affirm this expectation by treating them already as brothers and sisters too. Of course, this pushes us to the thorny problem of the enemy, whom I have to love according to the same Sermon on the Mount, but whom I cannot love, because I have no experience of the enemy's love, because therefore I cannot recognize him or her as brother or sister. And this enemy is in this case not only a private opponent. It is a massive representative of a godless and misanthropic system, profiteer of that anthropology of the solitary human, who fears to lose all with the downfall of this system. Whoever sets out on the journey of love, therefore, will find opposition and will be involved in struggles, in which he or she can become lonely, but not on account of the anthropology of the solitary human, but because of his/her resistance against it as followers of the lonely crucified one of Golgotha. Therefore they will not let the enmity of the enemy be victorious over them so much that they leave the way of their journey. They will love the enemy above all in this form that they, *instead of him*, quasi as his representatives, love the one who does not love, because he tramples them down: his victims. They show with this that they love exactly in this way also the enemy himself, that they don't identify him with his enmity by avoiding being infected with his hostility, that by not sanctioning it, they will not buy it, as Dietrich Bonhoeffer said. And this way they wait so that even the enemy will become perceptible as a brother or sister. Thus also, in this ethically extreme case of love, we cannot renounce its mutuality, because it is right that in the act of true love I can't alone play the active part, while the other is only the passive object of my love-duty. For then I pretend that it is only the other who needs me, while I for myself don't need them. However, there is also on the human level no loving without being loved. In order to love I am dependent on others who help and allow me to be their fellow human and neighbour. They are in the first place not law, nor duty, but gift. With nothing more I respect their human dignity in this, that they, in their 'otherness,' are welcoming to me. Yves Congar speaks of the 'sacrament of the neighbour',[30] that is the visible sign of the invisible grace. So they help me to become a human, who is a fellow human, even a brother or a sister with them. In this context what Emanuel Levinas said is true: 'that my self-esteem depends on it, whether others can rely on me'.[31] Such a mutual love is the practice of that community, of which I wanted to speak here, in order to show its importance in the present and for the future.

Notes

1   *Heidelberger Katechismus*, Fr. 104.
2   *Die Bekenntnisschriften der reformierten Kirche,* Leipzig 1903, hg. E. F. K. Müller, 30. Vgl. Kap. 3.
3   *Heidelberger Katechismus*, Fr. 54.

4 *Heidelberger Katechismus*, Rev., Fr. 33. Cf. *Genfer Katechismus* (1545), Fr. 46 f.

5 J. Calvin, *Institutio*, IV.i.3.

6 *Emdener Katechismus* (1554), Fr. 47, hochdeutsch übersetzt nach: *Bekenntnisschriften*, hg. E. F. K. Müller, 674.

7 *Heidelberger Katechismus*, Rev., Fr. 55.

8 *Westminster Confession of Faith*, Kap. 26,1, nach: *Bekenntnisschriften*, hg. E. F. K. Müller, 599.

9 J. Calvin, *Institutio*, III.ii.41–4.

10 *Heidelberger Katechismus*, Rev., Fr. 123.

11 J. Calvin, *Institutio*, IV.xvii.38.

12 R. Descartes, *Discours de la méthode* (1637), IV,3.

13 F. Nietzsche, *Ecce homo. Also sprach Zarathustra*, in: ders., *Werke in drei Bänden*, Bd. 2, München 1960, 1135.

14 J. G. Fichte, *Die Bestimmung des Menschen* (1800), in: ders., *Ausgewählte Werke*. Bd. 3, Hamburg 1962, 320–22.

15 R. Descartes, *Discours*, VI,3.

16 V. Forrester, *Der Terror der Ökonomie*, Wien 1997, 15.

17 G. Anders, *Die Antiquiertheit des Menschen*, Bd. 2, München 1995 (4. Aufl.), 15–33.

18 K. Barth, *Kirchliche Dogmatik*, IV/2, 474.

19 Ortega y Gasset, *Der Aufstand der Massen*, Hamburg 1956, 41.

20 R. Sennett, *Der flexible Mensch. Die Kultur des neuen Kapitalismus* (E.T.: *The Corrosion of Character*), Berlin 1998, 198.

21 P. Virilio, *Die Sehmaschine*, Berlin 1989; ders., *Sehen ohne zu sehen*, Bern 1991; ders., *Das öffentliche Bild*, Bern 1992. Vgl. Kap. 7.

22 P. Singer, *Wie sollen wir leben? Ethik in einer egoistischen Zeit*, München 1999, 263.

23 G. Gutiérrez, *Der Ausgegrenzte wird zum Jünger*, in: Concilium 30 (1994): 356 f.

24 R. Sennett, (Anm. 29), 198.

25 J. Habermas, *Die Einbeziehung des Anderen. Studien zur politischen Theorie*, Frankfurt 1997 (2. Aufl.), 57 f.

26 *Ibid.*, Ebd., 17.

27 *Ibid.*, Ebd., 58.

28 K. Barth, *Kirchliche Dogmatik*, III/2, 272.

29 M. Buber (*Dial. Prinz.*, 7).

30 Y. Congar, *Vaste monde ma paroisse: Vérité et dimensions du Salut* (E.T.: *The Wide World My Parish: Salvation and its Problems*), Paris 1959, 144.

31 R. Sennet, *Der flexible Mensch*, 200 (citing Levinas).

8

SOLI DEO GLORIA?
Divine Sovereignty and Christian Freedom in the 'Age of Autonomy'

Colin Gunton

I *Identifying the problem (1): The glory of God*

To begin with two Old Testament allusions. I recall from many years ago Eric Heaton's Oxford lectures on the prophets. He had clearly taken a dislike to the preoccupation of Ezekiel, that austere Barthian, with the glory of God's name, that apparent self-preoccupation of God which appeared so questionable to him. It is, however, a feature of the Old Testament's God that he is 'jealous,' intolerant of all rivals, and in view of the grim harvest of the semi-Marcionism and covert anti-semitism of so much of the Christian tradition, we ignore it at our peril. We shall not develop an adequate theology unless we can at least do justice to this side of the Bible's characterisation of the God of Israel, rounded off as it is in the work of Ezekiel's greatest disciple, the author of the Apocalypse. There we are reminded of the eschatological perfection of the divine glory: 'The city does not need the sun or the moon to shine on it, for the glory of God gives it light, and the Lamb is its lamp' (Rev 21:23). Nor should we forget that one of scripture's greatest ascriptions of glory to God is to be found in the completion of Paul's treatment in Romans 11 of the eschatological reconciliation of Jew and Gentile in obedience to the one God of them all.

A second allusion reinforces the point. 'God behaves like the crabby old cuss that we know Him to be'.[1] If we are to be true to scripture, we may not forget that the God of the Old Testament is the God of Jesus Christ, and the God of the Old Testament is not to be mocked. He has the first and last word, even though he allows his friends, quintessentially Abraham, much scope for argument on the way. Robert Jenson is right. If we look here, at the God of Israel, we have a God among whose essential attributes is jealously. He will not tolerate from Israel, or anyone else, worship of anyone or anything else. 'He who sits in the heavens laughs; the Lord has them in derision' (Ps 2:4). There is much competition in recent theology among the candidates for what is the essence of sin, whether it be pride, violence, or, as in some feminist ripostes to this supposedly male preoccupation, a failure – and I parody – to value oneself adequately. In their different ways these all tend, when stated so baldly, to construe the matter non-relationally, as symptoms merely, and there is a case for saying that for scripture the disrupted relation to God, on which all depends, is best understood in terms of idolatry, the worship of gods, people – including and quintessentially the self – or things rather than and above their creator.

We should not, I believe, or not yet, construe this zeal for the honour of God's name merely anthropocentrically, as though God's jealously of all rivals is primarily expressed in terms of human interest: he is jealous so that we should not display the symptoms which so radically disrupt our life on earth. The God of Deuteronomy, of the prophets and the psalmists – to take just some examples – is intrinsically jealous of any rival, intrinsically the one God who will tolerate no rival. Those who forget this, or attempt to live as if it were not so, simply deceive themselves. We should not therefore necessarily take offence when Calvin makes God's glory one of the bases of his justification of the sinner. 'Do you see that the righteousness of God is not sufficiently set forth unless he alone be esteemed righteous, and communicate the free gift of righteousness to the undeserving? ... For, so long as man has anything to say in his own defense, he detracts somewhat from God's glory.'[2] (For Calvin, that is not the whole story, and the matter is held in dialectical relation with the outcome of such a stance, 'that our consciences in the presence of his judgement should have peaceful rest and serene tranquillity'; yet the dialectic is rightly not resolved into a claim that the divine glory is there for the sake of the peaceful conscience. It is to be celebrated for its intrinsic reality, because God is God.)

Yet it is also easy to turn our God into a devil. This has been the accusation sometimes levelled against the God of certain forms of predestinarian Calvinism – that he is in some way directly responsible for the Holocaust – and even, as in Barth's famous turning of his own categories against Schleiermacher, the God on whom we are absolutely dependent. Does God glory in the death of the sinner? For some, so it would seem, as in Jonathan Edwards' famous piece of rhetoric and in the enthusiasm of some modern Calvinists to ensure that hell is not empty: 'By the decree of God, for the manifestation of His glory, some men and angels are predestinated unto everlasting life; and others foreordained to everlasting death.'[3] Whatever we make of this, it is difficult to square with the eschatological visions of Romans 8 and Ephesians 1. And yet, without conceding anything to Westminster's prelapsarian ordination of personal creatures to the cosmic bonfire, we cannot, on the basis of scripture, accept an axiomatic universalism either. As in all theology, there is a fine line to be drawn somewhere, and here it is between, on the one hand, turning God into a self-obsessed tyrant, and, on the other, a liberal sentimentalism which refuses to acknowledge that God's glory and the perfection of his creation may involve the eschatological violence to which Miroslav Volf has so finely drawn attention:

> … it takes the quiet of a suburban home for the birth of the thesis that human nonviolence corresponds to God's refusal to judge. In a scorched land, soaked in the blood of the innocent, it will invariably die. And as one watches it die, one will do well to reflect about many other pleasant captivities of the liberal mind.[4]

Is modern suspicion of the affirmation that all things should serve the glory of God, and specifically its taking shape in the claim of the Westminster Shorter Catechism that 'the chief end of man' is 'to glorify God and to enjoy him for ever', one of those captivities? We shall return to the question, but first we must explore the other pole of our topic.

II *Identifying the problem (2):*
The limitations of freedom according to the Reformed tradition

Calvin's account of human moral and religious slavery is directly in the tradition of Augustine and the Luther of *The Bondage of the Will*. Yet the modern world represents the triumph of Erasmus, in a form, however, that he is unlikely to have relished. The situation, accordingly, is as follows: that in aiming for human liberation in terms of liberation from God, the modern world has constructed a prison for the spirit – I allude to Tolkien's reply to the charge of escapism, that if you are in jail, escape is scarcely to be refused – such that the cure is worse than the disease. There are, to be sure, a number of sides to modern 'liberalism.' One of them is that its concern for freedom surely echoes that of scripture, and might indeed to be understood as a challenge to Christians, in an age when the gospel appeared to have been distorted into a tool of repression, to organise themselves according to their own standards. We are, however, at present experiencing the other side of the matter, because if anything is evident at the present time it is that the arrogation of freedom has engendered the most frightful slaveries, whether in the violent history of our century or in the disastrous social and personal effects of the modern myth of self-realisation.

The questions are those of the meaning and source of autonomy. What is the most proper law of our own being, and how is it realised? At the extremes, we are faced with an absolute contrariety: either our autonomy comes from God, because he is the creator and redeemer from whom *all* dimensions of our being and action derive; or it comes from ourselves, because anything else would be a violation of our personal *Selbständigkeit* – a better word than 'independence' in this context. But the preference for the German word indicates that the matter is far less simple than a mere opposition, because the doctrine of creation implies a *relative* independence of the world from God, and the doctrine of the image of God perhaps something still greater in the case of the human creation. The doctrine of the Fall complicates the matter still further, especially for our Augustinian and Reformed tradition, because it implies something about the radical incapacitation and corruption of both human and nonhuman created reality: a – relative or radical – loss of freedom in fact.

Let us review three classic analyses of human incapacity from representatives of, and in the third case someone influenced by, the Reformed tradition. Calvin's treatment of "The Knowledge of God the Redeemer in Christ", which is the second book of his *Institutio*, is introduced with an extended treatment of that universal human bondage which is theologically described as sin. In opposition to mediaeval semi-Pelagianism, he contends that sin is an unavoidable derangement of that which is natural. Of relevance for our enquiry is the fact that for him it deprives human beings of freedom. The subtlety of Calvin's discussion is remarkable, for in it he is able to do justice at once to the depth of human bondage and to the freedom of God the Holy Spirit despite the opposition to enable human science, art and political order. The bondage is entered into freely, yet in such a way that freedom is lost. Calvin quotes Augustine's definitive analysis: "'Through freedom man came to be in sin, but the corruption which followed as punishment turned freedom into necessity.'"[5] The crucial distinction is between necessity and compulsion.

> Now, when I say that the will bereft of freedom is of necessity either drawn or led into evil, it is a wonder if this seems a hard saying to anyone, since it has nothing incongruous or alien to the usage of holy men. But it offends those who know not how to distinguish between necessity and compulsion.

What is noteworthy is that this distinction is justified by a *theological* analogy which shows the conceivability of the compatibility of necessity and freedom:

> … from His boundless goodness comes God's inability to do evil[.] Therefore if the fact that He must do good does not hinder God's free will in doing good … who shall say that man therefore sins less willingly because he is subject to the necessity of sinning?[6]

Just as, we might say, God's necessary doing of the good is a function of his being what he is – of his ontology – so the human necessity to sin derives from the human condition of universal fallenness.

It is important to note here that Calvin does not deny the continuing reality of the will. Here his authorities are Augustine and Bernard, showing that the Reformed tradition is here in complete continuity with aspects of its patristic and mediaeval inheritance. 'For man, when he gave himself over to this necessity, was not deprived of will, but of soundness of will'. He cites Bernard's analysis at length:

> "Among all living beings man alone is free; and yet because sin has intervened he also undergoes a kind of violence, but of will, not of nature, so that not even thus is he deprived of his innate freedom. For what is voluntary is also free." And a little later: "In some base and strange way the will itself, changed for the worse by sin, makes a necessity for itself. Hence, neither does necessity, although it is of the will, avail or excuse the will, nor does the will, although it is led astray, avail to exclude necessity. For this necessity is as it were voluntary."[7]

We shall return to the relation of necessity and freedom, but must first engage with the Enlightenment's attempt to evade it.

By the time of Jonathan Edwards, Enlightenment thinkers – of whom he was one, as we must always remember[8] – had subjected the Augustinian and Calvinist philosophy of the will to sustained, if, as Edwards was to show, naïve analysis. His great treatise therefore enables us to enrich our picture of the human bondage which can be ended only by redemption. Edwards argues essentially that no willed act is without cause, so that to speak of absolute freedom, what he called freedom of indifference, is an absurdity: 'To suppose the will to act at all in a state of perfect indifference, either to determine itself, or to do anything else, is to assert that the mind chooses without choosing.'[9] For example, no consciously willed act is entered on without some motive, which thus operates *causally*.

> But if every act of the will is excited by a motive, then that motive is the cause of the act of the will. If the acts of the will are excited by motives, then motives are the cause of their being excited; or, which is the same thing, the cause or their being put forth into act and existence. And if so, the existence of the acts of the will is properly the effect of their motives. Motives do nothing as motives or inducements, but by their influence; and so much as is done by their influence is the effect of them. For that is the notion of an effect, something that is brought to pass by the influence of another thing.[10]

What Edwards demonstrates is that freedom is not the exercise of a will that is somehow other than the person as a whole. There is no 'inner person' or homunculus which is somehow a replica of the outer while being free (*sic*) from the outer's involvement in relations of influence and determination within the structures of worldly reality. The latter expression is perhaps a gloss or extension of the point Edwards is making about motivation, but it holds. Human beings are *creatures*: that is to say, beings whose reality is what it is by virtue of their interrelatedness in time and space with other creatures. The extent of the determination – whether it should be understood in terms of predestination or 'determinism' is here not to the point. What is relevant is that for the creature, caught up in a web of 'influences,' there simply is no undetermined act. If there is 'freedom' it must be understood within the terms of human creaturehood as it actually is, and the strength of Edwards' analysis is in part that it stands for the human condition in general, even had Adam not fallen.

At this stage we can pause to recall that Kant ('the century's coming to an understanding of itself – but of itself in its limitations'[11]) was aware enough of the problems involved to attempt to circumvent them. Unlike Edwards, however, he wishes to have his cake and eat it: to affirm determinism in a strong sense and an almost absolute freedom of will in parallel with it. His dialectic of inner moral freedom and outer determinism is an evasion of the problem, as later debate – even until today – has demonstrated beyond peradventure. Yet Kant's awareness of the age's limitations involved a contempt for a mere moral optimism which drove him deeper. His doctrine of radical evil ('Is it possible with impunity to be so far in agreement with St Paul as Kant after all was in his doctrine of sin?'[12]) laid the ground for an analysis not simply of the constitution of the will in its relationship with its creator and its situatedness in the web of creaturely existence, but of its bondage. This bore fruit in the nineteenth century in a deepening of the analysis of the psychological realities which underlie Calvin's dialectic of necessity and freedom.

Coleridge's account, aided as it was by both his engagement with Kant and his entrapment in addiction to drugs enables us to penetrate further into the well-springs of the slavery that is sin. Before citing Coleridge's penetrating analysis, it is worth pausing to say how much we owe here to recent explorations of character, virtue and *habitus* which enable a realisation that we are who and what we *particularly* are in large measure as the result of the way in which we are both made and make ourselves by our moral formation and the acts which contribute to it. While Schleiermacher's doctrine of sin in other respects can be argued to underestimate the depth of the human plight, he is perceptive on its social dimensions:

> Whether ... we regard it as guilt and deed or rather as a spirit and a state, it is in either case common to all; not something that pertains severally to each individual and exists in relation to him by himself, but in each the work of all, and in all the work of each; and only in this corporate character, indeed, can it be properly and fully understood. ... the aggregate power of the flesh in its conflict with the spirit ... is intelligible only by reference to the totality of those sharing a common life ...[13]

Schleiermacher's great contemporary knew something more profound about both the guilt and the slavery which his sin involved, and his perceptiveness advances our argument:

By the long habit of the accursed Poison my Volition (by which I mean the faculty *instrumental* to the Will, and by which alone the Will can realise itself – its Hands, Legs & Feet, as it were) was completely deranged, at times frenzied, dissevered itself from the Will and became an independent faculty: so that I was perpetually in the state, in which you may have seen paralytic Persons, who attempting to push a step forward in one direction are violently forced round to the opposite. I was sure that no ease, much less pleasure, would ensue: nay was certain of an accumulation of pain. But tho' there was not prospect, no gleam of Light before, an indefinite indescribable Terror as with a scourge of ever restless, ever coiling and uncoiling Serpents, drove me on from behind.[14]

The distinction between the will – that personal centre which we have seen Bernard and Calvin to maintain even after the fall – and the volition – the will in operation – enables us to see something of the psychological shape of the bondage. Coleridge's radical reappropriation of the above cited saying of Calvin, 'For man, when he gave himself over to this necessity, was not deprived of will, but of soundness of will', may appear to characterise the deeply wicked and addicted, and not be generalisable to the human situation as a whole. But two recent analyses of sin in relation to the modern evasion of the reality universal human fallenness have reminded us that it is a difference of degree, not kind. Miroslav Volf's response to the travails of Croatia has demonstrated that in this conflict no one is free from at least a measure of guilt. The crisis is a demonstration of the lost human condition as a whole: 'A particular evil not only "inhabits" us so that we do what we hate (Romans 7:15); it has colonized us to such a thoroughgoing extent that there seems to be no moral space left within the self in which it could occur to us to hate what we want because it is evil'.[15] The language of colonisation is the language of enslavement by something that takes away autonomy. Similarly, one of the strengths of Cornelius Plantinga's recent *Not the Way It's Supposed to Be: A Breviary of Sin*[16] is that it shows that the modern arrogation of freedom is in fact a form of displacement, so that what we take to be freedom in the modern world is in fact a radical form of slavery. When God is displaced by the human will, what eventuates is not freedom but all kinds of self- (and other-) destructive activity and attitudes. And the point does not apply simply to the social and psychological realms, but to our interaction with the broader environment. Our arrogation of absolute freedom distorts our relation with the whole universe:

In order to generate reliable policies of action the modern rhetoric of absolute freedom requires comprehensive knowledge of all these aspects of action. But, in fact, our knowledge is limited. It is not only quantitatively limited, but qualitatively limited in that it is mediated through our social forms of existence and the physical processes of our interaction with our environment. The modern rhetoric of freedom persuades us to ignore these limitations of our action-directing knowledge systematically ...[17]

This almost universal modern syndrome can only be understood theologically, in terms of that fundamental disorientation of the human relation to God that is sin, and quintessentially the sin of idolatry, for the ideology *of* absolute freedom is but a way of playing God. Edwards' description of what he calls the Arminian conception of freedom could be a description of God's:

... a self-determining power in the understanding, free of all necessity; being independent, undetermined *by* anything prior to its own acts and determinations; and the more understanding is thus independent, and sovereign over its own determinations, the more free.[18]

Edwards knew, without benefit of the destructive realities which this conception has helped since his time to generate, that it was simply mistaken:

Certainly, this no liberty that renders persons the proper subjects of persuasive reasoning, arguments, expostulations, and suchlike moral means and instruments ... according to this, the more free men are, the less they are under the government of such means, less subjects to the power of evidence and reason, and more independent on their influence ...[19]

In a many respects, to be sure, none of this is original. What gives it its power is the fact that a highly persuasive account of the modern doctrine of the individual freedom of indifference suggests that it is tantamount to the Augustinian-Reformed doctrine of sin, and the plausibility of that is reconfirmed by the crisis of modern social and international order, if such it can be said to be. And what makes the account even more persuasive is that however paradoxical the Reformed view may appear to be, its paradox derives more from the complexities of the relation between God and his creatures than that of its rival, which derives from the inherent contradictions of the liberal position.

III *The double mistake of modern 'liberalism'*

In sum so far: modern liberalism fundamentally misconstrues the human condition, in both its createdness and its fallenness, confusing freedom and sin. A move to a re-establishment of a properly theological and Reformed doctrine of freedom will require at least the following.

First, created freedom is not only compatible with, but actually requires constraint if it is to be genuinely a freedom of the creature. Jeremy Begbie has made the point with respect to music, that the freedom of improvisation is dependent on a high degree of cultural constraints, in this case 'the given musical material and strategies which shape it'.[20] Music, as the supremely temporal art, reminds us of the fact that we are shaped and formed in time, as the allusion above to *habitus* makes clear. Begbie cites John Webster's comment on Barth's conception of the moral agent to the effect that by constraint is here meant not 'confinement' but 'specificity' or 'particular shape':

> At first blush, 'limitation' suggests 'confinement', whereas Barth means something closer to 'specificity' or 'particular shape'. The human creature is limited ... in the sense that it is not an indeterminate, quasi-infinite moral self; but its limitedness by God is not its being hemmed in by an alien will, but rather its formation into *this* good creature.[21]

Particularity in time and space is here central. The material bodies in which we are born move inexorably to death, and it is what happens to and is made of that embodiedness which determines who and what we are, not some intellect and will which are somehow separate from and above them. (That is not to suggest that they do not transcend them; the problem with what for the sake of argument I am parodying as liberalism is that it abstracts, or attempts to abstract, this transcendence from material entanglements.) Similar considerations apply to our spatiality, with especial reference to the limitations of our knowledge which are referred to in the citation from Christoph Schwöbel above. It is important to remember that this is not a curse but a blessing. Human createdness and particularity are the gifts of God, and liberate us to be the particular selves, the particular men and women we are, children of particular parents and bound up with particular family, friends, colleagues and above all fellow members of the body of Christ, aspects of whose human journey we have been elected to share. To need to be God, to have to make ourselves, is not a freedom, but a terrible slavery, as our world is discovering to its cost. As tradition- and community-dwelling beings, we have the accumulated wisdom of the ages and the love of our various fellow men and women on which to call, and this is liberating because it is what it means to be human. But there is a darker side, and to this we turn.

Second, being sinful human beings means, as we have seen, being entrapped in social arrangements and bodies which bear the marks of a deep and inherited corruption, handed on inexorably from generation to generation. If it is not the case, as is sometimes claimed, that the doctrine of original sin is the one demonstrable article of Christian belief – not, because the relation to God which determines it is not demonstrable – then something like it is. As we have seen, it is a mark of Kant's greatness that even this believer in the absoluteness of human freedom held that moral optimism was in face of the actual facts an absurdity. It follows that there is freedom for the human moral agent only in being set free. 'Where the Spirit of the Lord is, there is freedom' (2 Cor 3:17), clearly means in its context that only through reconciliation with God the Father through the substitutionary death of his incarnate Son Jesus is the proper human particularity – right relation to God, the neighbour and the world – restored by reorientation to the eschatological perfection that is the promise of human being in the world. It is in this light only that we return to the theology of the glory of God, something, it is to be noted, highly prominent in the passage from 2 Corinthians that has formed the background to the theology of this paragraph.

IV *A defence of the* soli Deo gloria

As we have already implicitly seen, it is a mistake to apply in a univocal manner the doctrine of the image of God. To say that the freedom of the human being is only freedom if it is undetermined is in effect to apply a particular concept of divine freedom uncritically to the human case. (We might even ask whether the attribution of an essentially Ockhamist concept of freedom as absolute self-determination to God ignores the fact that God the Father's act is determined by the fact that he is the Father of the Son in the communion of the Holy Spirit; as we have seen Calvin saying, God is necessarily unable to do evil and so not *absolutely* free). One of the most foolish theological *dicta* ever to be uttered and given wide currency by vain repetition is that, 'if God is male, then the male is God.' It is both logically inconsequential and theologically false. Quite apart from the dubious assumption implicit in the hypothetical, it is by no means evident that the consequent follows.

In our context, the conclusion is to be drawn that divine self-glorification may be considered to be legitimate in a way that human self-glorification is not. (I say 'may' because we have not yet discussed what form such self-glorification may and may not take.) Steve Holmes makes a similar point with reference to Edwards: 'In *Two Dissertations*, which he left on his desk when he died, Edwards made the point: only God can be God without becoming demonic.'[22] Here I refer again to Miroslav Volf's point about violence. It by no means follows that the conceivability of divine (eschatological) violence undermines the validity of an ethic of non-violence.[23] We must hold on to this if we are not to minimize the seriousness of sin and evil by sentimentalizing God's way of dealing with it, which is by the cross. We might put the two aspects together by saying that human self-glorification is the root of sin, because it is precisely that which ignores and therefore distorts and disrupts the teleology and so the *being* of the created order. Calvin was not so wrong in characterising sin as pride because it is in pride that human beings aspire to being that which they are not created to be. Barth's point about the root of all sin – that 'man wants to be his own judge' – is to the same effect.[24] To grasp at human glory is to exchange the glory of God for a lie.

The heart of the matter of human sin is that it is self-centred and individualistic. Might it not appear that this is the case with God, also? Indeed on some conceptions that would be a justified charge.

> On the basis of a unipersonalist understanding of God the statement [that creation exists to glorify God] would indeed come close to theological catastrophe. It is here that the understanding of God as the triune Creator introduces quite a different perspective. ... on the basis of a trinitarian understanding of God, glory is not a self-directed attitude, but the mutuality of glorifying the other and receiving glory from the other which constitutes the communion of the divine life. Trinitarian glory is communicating glory and communicated glory.[25]

We now come to a second point. On a Trinitarian understanding, there is not, in God's case as there is in the human, a contradiction between the seeking of glory and the love of the other. God's actions in the world, as the overflow of his eternal triune glory into the order of time and space, are intrinsically other-directed. 'Father, the hour has come. Glorify your Son, that the Son may glorify you' (John 17:1). It is of the essence of the three persons of the Trinity that they give glory to one another, and what is true of the eternal being of God is also the case with the divine actions *ad extra*.

By what means does God glorify himself in the economy of his acts towards and in the world? Not only, we must say, by the weakness of the cross, but by the whole economy of what Barth summarised as creation, reconciliation and redemption: that is to say, in the beginning, middle and end of God's acts in towards and in the order of time, as its creator, redeemer and perfecter. The way in which, however, we construe that is determinative for the way we conceive of God's glory. First, we must say that the glory of God is simply what the creation is for. It is created *in order* to return God's goodness and giving in joyful praise: praise of words, works and life. That God glories in the praise of his creatures is in itself no more objectionable than that an orchestra glories in the applause of its audience. Irenaeus's much cited saying that 'the glory of God is a human being truly alive' is here very much to the point.[26] But, second, as we have seen, apart from reconciliation with the creator, there is only death – unfreedom consisting in a slavery to that which is not God, by virtue of sin. Reconciliation is at the heart, because there the false exchange (Romans 1) is displaced by the 'blessed exchange' of the cross, as the wider context of Ephesians makes manifest. When John's Jesus speaks of his 'lifting up' or glorification, reference is made to the cross, but also of the whole gamut of action and passion by which Jesus moves from the incarnation of the eternal Word to his ascension and mediation of the life-giving Spirit. One could here cite Eph 1:3–10 *in extenso*. God is praised, given glory, because he has chosen his people, both Jew and Gentile, to serve his purpose, realised in the blood of the cross, finally 'to bring all things in heaven and on earth together under one head, even Christ' (Eph. 1:10). It follows that freedom is an eschatological concept, realisable only where the Spirit brings people and things into right relation with God – not exclusively in those who consciously praise him, as we have seen Calvin affirming: 'The Lord is the Spirit, and where the Spirit of the Lord is there is freedom.'

The paradox of anthropocentrism is that that which seeks human glory denies both it and God's. 'In the mystery of God's providence, those who do seek the kingdom find that various other flourishings often follow, but not when directly aimed at.'[27] Is it not the case that as the quality of Bach's music, as music, is enhanced by the fact that it was written to the glory of God, that of some pretentious modern humanistic mirror images, Strauss's *Also Sprach Zarathustra* for example,[28] is diminished as *music* because it displaces the praise that is due to God alone? Perhaps Forsyth's attack on modern anthropocentrism is even more to the point: 'There is even what we might call a racial egotism, a self-engrossment of mankind with itself, a naïve and tacit assumption that God were no God if he cared for anything more than he did for his creatures.'[29] In sum: it is where the Reformed tradition[30] flies in the face of what is dearest to modernity's heart that we find the very place where the modern world might find its most wholesome and edifying lesson. But let the last word be with the poet:

> He that to praise and laud thee doth refrain,
> Doth not refrain unto himself alone,
> But robs a thousand who would praise thee fain,
> And doth commit a world of sinne in one.[31]

Notes

1   Jonathan Keates, "God's tales of blood and thunder," *The Spectator*, 30 January 1999.

2   John Calvin, *Institutes of the Christian Religion* (ed. J. T. McNeill; trans. F. L. Battles; Library of Christian Classics, vols. 20 and 21; Philadelphia: Westminster Press, 1960), III.xiii.1, p. 763.

3   *Westminster Confession of Faith* (1646), III, iii.

4   Miroslav Volf, *Exclusion and Embrace: A Theological Exploration of Identity, Otherness and Reconciliation* (Nashville: Abingdon Press, 1996), 304.

5   *Institutes*, II.iii.5, p. 295.

6   *Ibid.*

7   *Ibid.*, p. 296, quoting Bernard, *Sermons on the Song of Songs* lxxxi.7.9.

8   Robert Jenson, *America's Theologian: A Recommendation of Jonathan Edwards* (New York and Oxford: Oxford University Press, 1988).

9   Jonathan Edwards, *A Careful and Strict Enquiry into the Modern Prevailing Notions Of That Freedom of Will, Which is Supposed to Be Essential to Moral Agency, Vertue and Vice, Reward and Punishment, Praise and Blame* (ed. Paul Ramsey; New Haven and London: Yale University Press, 1957), 198.

10 *Ibid.*, 225.

11 Karl Barth, *Protestant Theology in the Nineteenth Century: Its Background and History* (trans. B. Cozens and J. Bowden; London: SCM Press, 1972), 266.

12 *Ibid.*, 297.

13 Friedrich Schleiermacher, *The Christian Faith* (ed. H. R. Mackintosh and J. S. Stewart; Edinburgh: T. & T. Clark, 1928), 288.

14 Cited by Richard Holmes from S. T. Coleridge, *Letters III*, pp. 189–90, in *Coleridge: Darker Reflections* (London: HarperCollins, 1998), 356 f.

15 Volf, *Exclusion and Embrace*, 89 f.

16 Cornelius Plantinga, *Not the Way It's Supposed to Be: A Breviary of Sin* (Grand Rapids: Eerdmans, 1995).

17 Christoph Schwöbel, "Imago Libertatis: Human and Divine Freedom," in *God and Freedom: Essays in Historical and Systematic Theology* (ed. Colin E. Gunton, Edinburgh: T. & T. Clark, 1995), 57–81, p. 66.

18 Edwards, *Freedom*, 223. As we shall see, such a conception is not even to be attributed to God.

19 *Ibid.*, 223 f.

20 Jeremy Begbie, *Theology, Music and Time* (Cambridge: Cambridge University Press, 2000).

21 John Webster, *Barth's Ethics of Reconciliation* (Cambridge: Cambridge University Press, 1995), 71. Cited in Begbie, *Ibid.*, 122.

22 Steve Holmes, "Edwards on the Will," *International Journal of Systematic Theology* 1 (1999): 266–85, p. 273.

23 See above note 4.

24 Karl Barth, *Church Dogmatics*, IV/1, 220.

25 Christoph Schwöbel, "God, Creation and the Christian Community: The Dogmatic Basis of a Christian Ethic of Createdness," in *The Doctrine of Creation: Essays in Dogmatics, History and Philosophy* (ed. Colin E. Gunton; Edinburgh: T. & T. Clark, 1997), 149–76, p. 169.

26 Irenaeus, *Against the Heresies*, 4.20.7.

27 Plantinga, *Not the Way It's Supposed to Be*, 38.

28 On British television, appropriately chosen to accompany broadcasting of one of the most futile of modern enterprises, the landing on the moon.

29 P. T. Forsyth, *The Person and Place of Jesus Christ* (London: Independent Press, 1946), 11. I thank Justyn Terry for this reference.

30 In the later published version of this conference paper Gunton changes 'the Reformed Tradition' here to 'the gospel': see C. E. Gunton, *Intellect and Action* (Edinburgh: T. & T. Clark, 2000), 173.

31 George Herbert, "Providence".

9

THE TRINITY:
On Observing a Proper Reserve –
Or On Not Claiming to Know Too Much!

PETER McENHILL

What constitutes a proper reserve in relation to the doctrine of the Trinity? The most famous or perhaps infamous expression of reserve is, of course, that of Schleiermacher who, at the close of his great work *The Christian Faith*, asserts that the doctrine of the Trinity 'is not an immediate utterance of the Christian self-consciousness but only a combination of several such utterances.'[1] The essential claim involved is to state that the being of God (the divine essence) is in Christ and in the Spirit indwelling the Church.[2] However, although these claims constitute the 'coping stone' of the Christian faith, we cannot from them posit an eternal distinction in the divine essence.[3] In attempting to posit such eternal distinctions in the divine essence the history of Trinitarian reflection reveals a deep instability, forever being unable to settle between the Scylla of modalism and the Charybdis of tri-theism. And the fact of this instability (according to Schleiermacher) shows the need for a reformulation of the doctrine from the roots up, and that such a reformulation is called for is perhaps the unfinished theological work of the emergent churches of the Reformation.[4] The twentieth-century focus upon the centrality of the doctrine of the Trinity for the whole enterprise of theology – a strong feature of, but certainly not exclusive to, the theological work of Reformed and Protestant theologians – could be viewed as some sort of fulfillment of Schleiermacher's prophecy, although the fulfillment, coming as it has in the prevailing tendency to stress the social, communitarian or (tritheistic?) dimensions of Trinitarian thought, is not perhaps what Schleiermacher (whose Sabellian sympathies are well known would perhaps have expected.

159

One of the briefs of this paper will be to suggest that rather than viewing the instability of the doctrine of the Trinity (if instability is the right word) as a problem, it may just be better to suggest that the oscillation between the two limiting poles of monotheism and tri-theism, the oscillation between unity in diversity and diversity in unity, just names the particular dialectic that is the Christian doctrine of the Trinity. Suggesting a partial (and I stress very partial) analogy from the field of quantum physics, we might suggest that the doctrine of the Trinity is analogous to the famous wave-particle duality that we hear so much about. That is to say, just as a physicist can ascertain the position of a particle, but can say virtually nothing about its momentum and vice versa, the theologian can similarly assert the absolute unity of the divine being, but cannot at the same time give a full and unambiguous account of the diversity of individual relationships and the precise particularity of the persons contained within the Godhead, or she can describe the diversity and particularity of the persons, but not at the same time get back to an unambiguous account of the unity of the Godhead. The Trinity as a quantum field if you like. (But this is no more than a wink or passing suggestion – a very vague allusion really.) I myself tend towards the unitive end of the pole for reasons that I will provide later, but that too is held with an appropriate degree of reserve. However, the instability or oscillation to which I have alluded does mark many recent and not so recent approaches to the doctrine of the Trinity and so perhaps some further examination of at least some of those accounts will be appropriate.

For the purposes of this volume it is worth pointing out that there has been a significant focus upon the doctrine of the Trinity in the works of many Reformed theologians of the twentieth century. Barth's monumental contribution of course, but Berkhof too, and Moltmann likewise have all made substantial contributions. And from the English-speaking sphere of the theological world there have been rich contributions from Gunton and Torrance[5] also. Schleiermacher's call for a re-examination of the doctrine has surely then not gone unanswered.

However, I wish to begin with a minor strand in that Anglophone take on the Trinity by considering D. M. Baillie's treatment of the doctrine in his famous work *God was in Christ*.[6] Baillie concludes his work on Christology with an attempt – in what is little more than a suggestive sketch really – to spell out the implications of his thought for the doctrine of the Trinity and in so doing he notes two divergent trends in contemporary (to him)

Trinitarian thought. He notes the tendency towards the 'modalistic' pole of Trinitarian thought in the writings of Karl Barth, and contrasts that with the 'social Trinitarian' position of Leonard Hodgson. Baillie was a relatively astute reader of Barth, noting that despite Barth's preferred use of the term 'modes of being' rather than persons, nevertheless Barth is not simply following in the Sabellian lines of Schleiermacher. Baillie follows Barth through the various lines of argument in *The Doctrine of the Word of God*, noting the rejection of three distinct centres of consciousness for the preferred formula that 'The God who reveals Himself according to Scripture is One in three of His own modes of existence, which consist in their mutual relationships, Father, Son, and Holy Spirit.' And that, 'It is to the one single essence of God, which is not to be tripled by the doctrine of the Trinity, but emphatically to be recognised in its unity, that there belongs what we call today the "personality" of God.'[7] Again, Barth elsewhere argues that, in the sense of which we speak of ourselves as persons it is better to think of God as one rather than three. Indeed God is the true and real person over against our sense of ourselves as persons. Summing up, Baillie quotes Barth (in a section that has much influenced Jenson) as saying,

> '... that those three elements are not foreign to the Godness of God. The relationship is not that we should have to seek the proper God beyond these three elements, in a higher being in which He was not the Father, the Son and the Spirit. The revelation of God, and therefore His being as Father, Son and Spirit, is not an economy foreign to His essence, limited as it were from above or from within, so that we should have to enquire about the hidden Fourth, in order to really inquire about God.'[8]

So far so not Moltmann.

Baillie is broadly appreciative of Barth's position, and indeed is closer to it than he is to Hodgson's social analogy, but he does, in anticipation of later theological estimates recognise that Barth's position can be read in the direction of a single unitary being.[9] Whilst sympathetically received, Hodgon's position is described as forming part of an ultra-Cappadocianism that describes the Trinity as a 'social unity.' Baillie notes the strongly related ethical and social implications of such an approach, focusing around the concept of God as social unity – a social organism inspired by Divine Love.[10]

However, in his own form of observing a proper reserve, Baillie does

not propose to attempt a settlement between the two types of Trinitarian
interpretation, suggesting – a little thinly – that different approaches to the
problem of the Trinity may be ultimate for different types of mind,[11] but he
does reveal that his preference lies definitively with Barth and with Barth
read more sympathetically than Moltmann would allow. Baillie approves of
Barth's statement:

> 'Even in the life of God within the Trinity, of course, the eternal generation
> of the Son or Logos is the expression of God's love, of His wish not to be
> alone. ... The eternal generation of the Son by the Father itself asserts first
> and foremost that even apart from the world and us altogether God is not
> lonely: His love has its object in Himself.'[12]

In response to Hodgson, Baillie argues that the social analogy (and for
Hodgson it is an analogy) is not finally adequate as the unity of three Persons
in God is a higher kind of unity than any other than we can imagine. However,
Baillie is forced from his posture of eirenic acceptance by asserting that in
Hodgon's postulating of three distinct personalities we seem to imply that
they are parts of God and it is difficult to get beyond this to some form of
unity.[13] For if they are distinct persons we have to ask in what sense they
might be limited by each other as finite persons? And if such a suggestion
is intolerable, what sense can we make of the opposite suggestion of three
infinite beings?[14] Baillie does not develop these points analytically (as Brian
Leftow does with the similar suggestions of Brown and Swinburne),[15] but
he does point out that the intellectual sources of the 'social Trinity,' i.e. the
Cappadocian Fathers, mitigated their stress on the diversity of the threeness
of the persons through the doctrine of *perichoresis*, and by their teaching
that the whole of God is in each of the three persons. Consequently, Baillie
understands that while those Fathers could speak of the Trinity under the
analogy of three individual men, they used the analogy only in a very limited
measure and did not go the whole way with the idea that the Persons are three
distinct personalities in a 'social unity' even of the highest kind.[16] Baillie
further points out that the term 'three modes of existence' is thoroughly
Cappadocian and that their strongest intent was always to stress the unity of
the divine *ousia* by virtue of their stress on the identity of operation of all
three divine persons.[17] The important aspect to mention here is that Baillie
apparently reads the Cappadocians very much in accord with the recent

reinterpretation offered by Sarah Coakley, Lewis Ayres, Lucian Turcescu, et al.[18] We will return to this in a moment, but I simply want to conclude that Baillie proceeds to illustrate the authentically Christian teaching of the Trinity by reference to the sending of Jesus and the experience of the Spirit in the Church so that,

> The New Testament can also speak of God the Father dwelling in Christ, and of the Holy Spirit being given to Christ; and it can speak of God the Father dwelling in us and we in Him, and of Christ dwelling in us, and we in Him. All this seems impossible to systematize until we remember the historical facts and experiences out of which it arose, and attempt to relate them to the eternal God. When we do that, the doctrine of the Trinity sums up the Gospel by telling us that the God of grace, who was revealed through the Incarnation and Pentecost as the One who paradoxically works in us what He demands of us, is the same from all eternity and for ever more'.[19]

So much for Baillie's position, but it would seem that the immediate judgement of theological history was not to be with him, for recent Trinitarian reflection has tended towards the social or communitarian tend of the spectrum in the writings of thinkers as diverse as Zizioulas, Moltmann, Gunton, Boff, Brown, Swinburne and Jenson – a formidable offensive line-up that would make even the most confident wary. The rationale for such approaches varies from an examination of the death of Christ as an event in the life of God, to an attempt to be more faithful to the broad sweep of the revelatory scriptural narrative, to the development of a more nuanced and relational understanding of the person via the writings of Macmurray, Webb and Buber and the locating of the origins of this development in the approach of the Cappadocian Fathers.

This position is usually contrasted sharply with the position ('supposed') of Augustine, who it is said never breaks from God as absolute subject, to Aquinas, who faithfully follows Augustine and whose relations of origin or opposition fails to provide real persons in the Godhead, or if it does so, only fails to produce a quaternity from the logic of the relations by sheer dictat.[20] It is also contrasted with the positions of Barth and Rahner, who, despite their excellent repositioning of the doctrine of the Trinity, are finally held to have succumbed to the Western tendency to understand God as an isolated absolute subject and thus to fail finally to offer a genuinely Trinitarian understanding of God.[21]

Baillie contrasts Barth's position with that of Leonard Hodgson (a committed 'social Trinitarian') who was bold enough to say of his own assessment of the historical treatment of the tradition, 'I am of the opinion that if St. Augustine, St Thomas and Calvin were alive to-day they would be glad in this respect to revise what they have written.'[22] Hodgson, does not quite read Augustine, Aquinas and Calvin as convinced 'social Trinitarians,' but he does believe that the difficulties inherent in their positions betray a tension between the abstract conceptualizations that they develop and the vivid reality of the loving communion between Father, Son and Spirit of which they were trying to write. Hodgson is clearly not willing to follow them down the route of metaphysical confusion for he confesses that he has 'no idea what generation or procession meant in relation to the persons of the Trinity, and therefore did not intend to waste time by treating of them'. Hodgson finds support for his reading of the tradition in Augustine's suggestion that the Trinity is lover, loved and love – although he notes that Augustine simply touches upon this idea and then moves on. However, in Book XV of *The Trinity*, Hodgson notes that Augustine points out the inadequacy of the analogy from the image of God that he had been developing. For,

> Whereas each man is one person, and the trinity which is the image is in his mind, the divine Trinity is God, and is not one but three Persons. ... Moreover we men only remember with the memory, know with the intellect, and love with the will; but in the divine Trinity each Person does all three ... each is complete, is memory, intellect and love.[23]

Hodgson notes that Augustine later repeats the point that whereas in each of us the analogous trinity exists in one person, the divine Trinity is a unity in which each member is a complete Person. Hodgson concludes,

> Whatever may be the etymological history of the words [*hypostasis*] and *persona*, it is impossible to avoid the conclusion that St. Augustine regarded each Person in the Godhead as being personal in whatever sense the word is used of conscious, intelligent and purposive human beings.[24]

For Hodgson then, revelation requires that the Trinity comprises each person as being fully personal in the modern sense of the word.[25] Where Hodgson parts company with Augustine is in the fact that Augustine accords primacy of place as the *principium* of divinity to the Father, and neither does he think that the terms 'filiation' or 'procession' speak of anything that may be called 'derivation' – a characteristic move perhaps of 'social approaches' to the Trinity.[26]

If Augustine implicitly regards each person in the Trinity as 'personal' in the sense of being conscious, intelligent and purposive beings, then it appears that Thomas must too, as, according to Hodgson, he essentially repeats, refines and clarifies Augustine's basic teaching. Hodgson again:

> The religion of St. Thomas is a full-blooded trinitarianism. In his theology he is wrestling to express this in terms of a philosophical notion of unity which cannot contain it. The result is that the abstract terms in which he attempts in the *Tractatus* to describe the relations of the divine persons appear somewhat like the "bloodless categories" of Bradley's famous phrase.[27]

Hodgson clearly sees Thomas as providing not a description of intra-Trinitarian life but a grammar of Trinitarian discourse that emerges from the fact of revelation. Like Augustine, imprisoning and alien philosophical categories distort and make lifeless what he intends to say about the living reality he encounters through faith.

> St Thomas surely never meant his theology to be used for the purpose of desiccating the revelation which God had given through the activity of Son and Spirit in the incarnation, the atonement and the continued life of the Church. Through that revelation he worshipped three Persons in one God. He sought, by logical analysis of the nature of being, to show how this could be, and how predicates could rightly be used of the Persons severally and of the Trinity as a whole. But the Persons themselves, though they might be thought and spoken of as existing in the five notions and the four relations, or power, wisdom and love, were always more than this. The living content of each was given by that which He made known of Himself to faithful worshippers.[28]

This is perhaps a slightly more generous assessment of at least the intent – if not completely of the result – of the Western tradition's sincere attempt to speak of a real plurality and diversity in the Trinity than is customary among contemporary 'social Trinitarians.'

To return to the Cappadocian Fathers – or at least Gregory of Nyssa – recent work in this area has suggested that the reading offered of this tradition by the various 'social or communitarian Trinitarians' is less than just to their intent. Thus Sarah Coakley points out, and here I summarise, that the famous analogy of the three men is not Gregory of Nyssa's, but is a given in the question of his opponent. That Gregory's normal insistence and prime emphasis is upon the divine unity (as a counteraction to late Arianism) and that his method for asserting this unity is always to stress the unified will and power of God's activity. (This we saw earlier was essentially Baillie's point.) Furthermore the *principium* of the Godhead is always the Father.[29] In a related introductory piece in an issue of *Modern Theology*, intending to 'toll the final funeral bell on a misreading of Gregory's trinitarianism', Coakley attempts to counter John Zizioulas' reading of the Cappaodicans by arguing that Zizioulas is overly influenced by the reading of Prestige who misreads the Cappadocians, and (following Turcescu) that Zizioulas further imports contemporary notions of the relational person gained via Buber and Macmurray back into the Cappadocian Fathers. Coakley's reading is supported by the detailed exegesis of the Cappadocian position found in three other articles in the same volume by Lewis Ayers, Lucian Turcescu and Michel René Barnes, whereas a fourth contributor to the collection (David Bentley Hart) draws attention to some profound similarities between Gregory and Augustine (so much so Hodgson). Together these essays constitute an attempt to counter the 'De Regnon' reading of Gregory of Nyssa and it is this reading which has directly influenced Lossky and Prestige and through them a host of others – most notably Zizioulas.[30] In addition to all these qualifications, Coakley is keen to stress the *apophatic* quality of the Cappadocian writings on the essence of God and to refute Zizioulas' contention that 'person precedes substance'.[31] As we have noted this is very similar to Baillie's brief reading, but also somewhat similar to a point made way back in 1954 by the late John McIntyre who took issue with both Prestige and Shapland's readings of the Cappadocians, as they, in various ways, suggested a secondary place for the unity of the divine substance in the order of thought of the Greek Fathers. According to McIntyre (anticipating Ayres and Coakley), the unity of the divine *ousia* is the primary axiom of the Fathers and the development of the term *hypostasis* was used to delineate, given this fundamental prior commitment to divine unity, the precise limits of our language for describing what are nevertheless real distinctions or individuations in the Godhead.[32] A similar point is made by James Mackey who, like Coakley, notes the stress on the ineffability and utter incomprehensibility of the divine essence in the Cappadocians and that this further reinforces the notion of an order of transmissions or *taxis* in the Trinity.[33] All powers being from the Father, advance through the Son and are completed by the Spirit – the divine action is one and is experienced as one – *à la* Schleiermacher. Hence we can begin to see why Coakley argues that communion rather than community is the better term for the Cappadocian description of God. Thus the fact that the Father is the source of the divinity and that the *hypostases* mutually indwell each other and have a complete unity of activity and intention is far removed from any notion – no matter how faint or dim the analogy might be held to be – of human community whether it be family, society or some other form of complex organism. It is still too early to say what the implications and consequences of this re-reading of the Cappadocians will be for those forms of 'social Trinitarianism' that have utilised Cappadocian thought as the presumed basis for their work, but they are likely to be significant. However, there are other forms of 'social Trinitarianism' that have not relied upon the Cappadocian model and these may continue to have value, and it is to one of the most famous of these that we now turn.

Jürgen Moltmann, of course, provides the supreme example of a 'social Trinitarianism' that does not depend upon the work of the Cappadocians.[34] (There is but one reference to Nazianzen in the entire text.) He famously rejects Barth's position as positing the Trinity of absolute subject, and also that of Rahner as positing God as three-fold self-communication.[35] Moltmann's 'social Trinity' is derived from the history of the biblical testimony and paradigmatically it is required by an explication of the cross as an event in God. Moltmann argues that God's passionate involvement with the world implies a self-differentiation in God himself.[36] This is easily the most powerful aspect of Moltmann's thought and it is one that challenges all presentations of the divine reality to take the cross seriously.

However, Moltmann never really offers a sufficiently rigorous conceptual analysis and description of the relationships of Father, Son and Holy Spirit as relationships of fellowship which are open to the world which would justify the claim to unity.[37] This allied to his suggestion (or inference) that somehow the triune God completes himself in the process of world history is a major weakness.[38] There is a major point at issue here and it is the issue of grace. For, whatever the demerits and limitations of God conceived as an impassible sole monarch of the world might be, it does at least have the virtue of stressing the utterly gracious nature of God's creative and redemptive action. If God needs nothing *extra se* to complete or enhance the divine life then all that has come into being has come into being through the sheer undetermined, unnecessary and un-coerced gratuitous act of God. However, if God achieves an eschatological 'self-deliverance from his sufferings' – even if God has voluntarily subjected himself to these sufferings – then surely an unanswerable question of theodicy inevitably arises? For, to put it crudely, if God gets something out of the deal, out of the processes of history, so to speak, if the divine life is enhanced or finds completion in some way, then we as the primary subjects of that history are entitled to ask questions about the sheer scale of the cost in human terms. Evil may finally be an unanswerable mystery within the traditional paradigm of an impassible unrelated creator, but at least therein the whole deal is something of a gratuitous 'free lunch' on God's part. More seriously perhaps, along with the vitiation of the language of grace, so also the notion of God's independent existence from the world is effectively nullified too in the idea that God is a reciprocal player or partner in the processes of history. For if there is any sense of reciprocity, if God 'needs' or 'achieves' something in the 'divine life' via the divine/human relationship, then it is no longer a relationship characterized solely by grace, but becomes a relationship in which God is in some degree – no matter even if only in an infinitesimally small way – a dependent partner. The effect is inevitably to reduce God to the status of another creature among creatures – a supercreature perhaps, but nevertheless a creature. The traditional assertions of the aseity, ineffability, incomprehensibility and impassibility of the Godhead are thus seen to be powerful strategies for avoiding precisely this conclusion.

That apart, if one gives up a prior commitment to divine unity why then – on the basis of the biblical data alone – would one interpret the cross of Christ as an event in the life of the one triune God? The New Testament nowhere offers as simple and as clear a portrayal of the triune relationships as Moltmann would like to think. Triads galore yes, but Trinitarian perichoretic relationships no. The history of modalism and subordinationism in the early centuries of the Church testify to the range of options that the basic scriptural affirmations might tentatively suggest. Similarly the recent (or relatively so) writings of critics of the classic Trinitarian doctrine such as Lampe and Wiles, testify to the range of interpretations that might be gleaned from the data of scripture and the early Fathers. Even the writings of much more cautious and orthodox scholars such as Moule and Dunn reveal a struggle to differentiate in the biblical data between the Spirit, the Spirit of Christ and the Spirit of God, or, at least, to differentiate in a manner that leads to a clear and unambiguous third person in the Trinity.

Moltmann's treatment of *hypostasis* and person is helpful but not sufficiently illuminating in that he says that 'the Son is the self-utterance of the Father and must not be conceived as again "uttering", and the Spirit is the "gift" which does not, in its turn, again give. God's self-communication occurs as the Father gives himself in absolute self-communication through the Son in the Holy Spirit. All this is fine (though not so distinct from the Western tradition as we might imagine) as is his assertion that,

> It is true that the Trinity is constituted with the Father as starting point, inasmuch as he is understood as being 'the origin of the Godhead'. But this 'monarchy of the Father' only applies to the *constitution* of the Trinity. It has no validity within the eternal circulation of the divine life, and none in the perichoretic unity of the Trinity.'[39]

And one is tempted to say here, how on earth could he or anyone else know that? The Cappadocian strictures on divine incomprehensibility come very much into view here. I am not quite sure what to make of this as I am not sure what Moltmann means by the 'constitution' of the Trinity by the Father. It rather sounds like the cranking up of a four-stroke piston engine, in that once God's Trinitarian life is kick-started, as it were, the process of *perichoretic* Trinitarian circulation begins. I am not completely unsympathetic to Moltmann's position and he does have some salient points to make about the Trinitarian tradition in the West, but one does wish he had attended to a more rigorous exegesis of the scriptural data and offered a tighter conceptual analysis of the personal relations than he has done. I think he is susceptible to Coakley's charge of assuming that person precedes substance rather than the fact that the two are inextricably intertwined. Given his preference for a divine fellowship of mutuality he does have to address, I am afraid, the type of questions that Leftow addresses to the similar positions of Brown and Swinburne.[40] Moreover, the suggestion that God completes himself in history, does tend to imply a certain essentialism to the world and its processes – including its evil processes – to the inner life of God and that should perhaps make us stop and ponder.

Similarly, his assertion that the portrayal of God as 'absolute subject' or as sole monarch has had deleterious effects upon human society is suggestive though not conclusively demonstrated. Moltmann asserts it rather than argues for it, and as has been said elsewhere there are many examples of three-man juntas which have been just as oppressive and coercive as sole monarchies. Indeed, Moltmann doesn't address the ways in which the growth of a single monarch or ruler in certain societies was a preferred option to the warlord banditry of multiple fiefdoms. A sole monarch often offered a limited and provisional form of order over against the chaos and anarchy of competing claims to power. As such monarchy may not be an absolute good, but a chaotic profusion of mini-monarchies is worse. Perichoretic Trinitarian accounts of the divine life cannot rightly be characterized as competing mini-monarchies of course (even though 'social Trinitarian' accounts of the matter might only do so by sheer assertion – for how might three infinite beings limit themselves?), but it is useful to remember that monotheism emerged out of polytheism in the Judaeo-Christian tradition. Historically speaking then it would seem that Trinitarianism needs the gravitational pull of an already existing absolute monotheism to emerge, whereas polytheism would always tend to resolve towards a true community of individual 'Gods'. Thus the assertion of the sole omnipotent power of Israel's God was developed in the face of polytheistic accounts of a profusion of sometimes warring deities and also over against competing dualisms. As such a simple baptising of the collective – as various forms of fascism demonstrate – will not solve the problems of sinful fragmented society. We must also remember, whenever we are tempted to offer the Trinitarian life as the model for human forms of communal living and being in the world, that Israel (and Islam too at its best) – with a profoundly monotheistic understanding of God – have been no less able to foster forms of communal life that lead to human flourishing and well-being. That is another form of reserve we should have in this regard.

I have already alluded to Brian Leftow's critique of 'social Trinitarianism' and would direct readers there for further examination of the issues involved, but simply wish to conclude by transposing a question from Bonhoeffer's christology to this issue and to reflect that perhaps most 'social Trinitarians' have been beguilled by the 'how' rather than the 'who' question. That is to say they attempt to show 'how' the Trinity 'works,' rather than being content to order appropriate Christian discourse concerning God so that the God portrayed in salvation history just is this God in his eternal life.

So in observing a proper reserve, I have tried to say that there should be a reserve in the complete rejection of one approach *vis-à-vis* the other. I myself tends towards one pole (the unitive – and in that regard I realize I may be held to be one of the failed and fabled 'functional unitarians'), but it is clear that both social and unitive models are much closer to each other than they are to anything else in their attempts to proclaim the differentiated unity that is the Christian God. This I hope was the point of considering Hodgson's treatment of Augustine and Aquinas from a 'social Trinitarian' perspective, but also too of the Coakley/Ayres reassessment of the Cappadocian position. There was, however, what we might term a prior Scottish (and for the purposes of this collection 'Reformed') reading of the tradition via Baillie and McIntyre that brought the Cappadocian understanding of the Godhead much closer to the themes and concerns of a supposedly opposite Western tradition.

There should also be a reserve on the part of those who have overly stridently sought to refute the supposedly Western bias towards a prior divine unity in the Godhead. We might ask if, without a prior commitment to divine unity and the unity of a personal act, there would have arisen the intense and exacting speculation that gave rise to the concept of a differentiated and complex yet somehow one being? Without the pull of that intense pole the scriptural narrative could and would so easily have been read in subordinationist or modalist terms. (As it was by so many in the second and third centuries – *à la* Justin Martyr and Origen.)

Perhaps there should also be a proper reserve because the current state of New Testament discussion does not allow us to move unproblematically from New Testament triads to a divine Trinity. The New Testament does not escape hierarchy and distinction if only because, historically and temporally speaking, sending and proceeding imply a derivative status. Appeals to the broad sweep of scriptural narrative and its implications for Trinitarian thought tend to ignore that it is only after many long battles had been won, and divine unity in Trinity had been clearly articulated dogmatically, that one can retroactively impose that pattern necessarily upon the New Testament itself. This would imply a reservation of judgment upon the writings of those like Lampe and Wiles, and even Schleiermacher, who are not at all convinced that the scriptural data furnish what we are after.

There should also perhaps be a certain reserve with respect to the use of terms such as 'person' and 'communion' (so much so Augustine and Barth). It is clear that when we use such language in relation to God we are stretching it analogically, metaphorically and paradoxically. Therefore to say that God is a person is to say that God is a person '*Trinitarianly conceived*' and in no other sense a person. Even if we wish to say that the Trinitarian personhood of God is the paradigmatic sense of what it is to be a person (as per Barth), we are still using 'person' in a different sense than when we apply it to an individual human being. Thus Michel Barnes, '... while Gregory may indeed be said to have a psychology of the Individuals of the Trinity, in the end that psychology maps out a radical difference between our self-experience and the "self-experience" of those Individuals.'[41] Barnes tellingly concludes his discussion by saying that,

> [Gregory's] true contribution to the discussion of psychology and Trinitarian theology may thus be to offer a reorientation of what should be discussed. Reading Gregory does not so much offer us opinions corresponding to an existing range of modern options, as it suggests that the very shape of what it means to use psychological terms in Trinitarian theology is different from modern expectations.[42]

For even if human personhood is conceived of as being thoroughly relationally and socially constituted it still remains true that I can be thought of as a person existing absolutely isolated and alone without any logical contradiction thereby being entailed. Psychologically, emotionally, socially and physically I might be a very much reduced 'person,' but I would remain nevertheless a person. I take it that much of the point of Trinitarian theorizing – both Western and Eastern – has been conducted precisely to show that the Divine persons, though distinguishable, cannot be conceived in absolute isolation one from another without logical contradiction. The Cappadocian image of pulling the links on a chain comes to mind here. To say that God is personal is one thing, but to say that God is a 'person' as we are persons *simpliciter* is to say something so different from the normal everyday use of that term that there should be a proper reserve in relation to its use.

Similarly, to say that God is a communion is to say that God is a communion '*Trinitarianly conceived*', and in no other sense a communion – and the language of *perichoresis* and mutual indwelling might just have alerted us to all of this in the first place. The value of those attempts to offer the divine inner life as some form of model for human forms of community is presumably put into question by the sheer difference between what we term the *perichoretic* community that is the Trinity and all of our forms of communal living. It is interesting to note that while the New Testament has much to say about how the Church as a community should live together, it rarely, if ever, offers the inner life of the immanent Trinity as a model or inducement as to how they should so live. Moreover, as we have already stated, it is the case that other monotheistic religious traditions have managed to create successful forms of human society and flourishing without having recourse to a Trinitarian understanding of the divine life. Perhaps this should alert us to the fact that human society is a gift and ordinance of creation and providential grace and thus the theological resources for developing benevolent forms of social life can be adequately rooted in those parts of the *loci* of the theological prospectus.

And reservations around this type of language might just have been the intent of the tradition after all? It was certainly the intent of John Robinson, who, in his Cambridge PhD thesis "Thou Who Art" develops an account of the human person following Buber, Ebner and Macmurray which understands the person as constituted in relation. Robinson's thesis predates much of the contemporary discussion offered by 'social Trinitarians' and Robinson locates the development of the concept of the term 'person' far more precisely in the Trinitarian disputes of the eighteenth and nineteenth centuries. However, despite his avowal of a relational understanding of the human person, and his account of the incarnation as God the Son constituting himself in the 'Thou' relation to God, he does not develop a relational account of the person of God. There is no (as there is in Moltmann and Jenson) retrojection from the temporal processions to the divine life. The external works of God are undivided and God is encountered in experience as the one God. In relation to the Trinitarian life of God, Robinson argues that God 'does not assert himself as a thou over against himself – that is a relation extra se.' He concludes his 600-plus page thesis thus,

> The revelation of the Trinity is but another way of stating the fact of the gospel. It is that which enables man to make the total response of faith and obedience to the One Lord of this life which is reconciliation and redemption ... If speculation on the nature of the Persons does not run into such acknowledgement and worship of a person, then it is clear that the Essence whose modes of being they are has been regarded as something other than the centre of consuming love which is the Christian God.[43]

This, I suspect, was also the intent of his near contemporary Baillie, and it is a fine example of a statement showing a proper reserve with respect to the persons of the Trinity.

Notes

1 F. D. E. Schleiermacher, *The Christian Faith*. Eng. trans. of the 2nd German ed. (ed. H. R. Mackintosh and J. S. Stewart; Edinburgh: T. & T. Clark, 1928) § 170, p. 738.
2 *Ibid.*
3 *Ibid.*, § 170:2, p. 739.
4 *Ibid.* § 172, p. 747.
5 Karl Barth, *Church Dogmatics*, I/1 *The Doctrine of the Word of God* (2nd Eng. ed., trans. G. W. Bromiley; ed. G. W. Bromiley and T. F. Torrance; Edinburgh: T. & T. Clark, 1975); Hendrikus Berkhof, *The Doctrine of the Holy Spirit* (London: Epworth Press, 1965); Jürgen Moltmann, *The Trinity and the Kingdom of God: The Doctrine of God* (trans. M. Kohl; London: SCM Press, 1980); Colin E. Gunton, *Father, Son and Holy Spirit: Essays Towards a Fully Trinitarian Theology* (London: T. & T. Clark, 2003); T. F. Torrance, *The Christian Doctrine of God, One Being Three Persons* (Edinburgh: T. & T. Clark, 1995).
6 D. M. Baillie, *God was in Christ* (London: Faber & Faber, 1948).
7 *Ibid.*, 135 f., citing Barth from *Church Dogmatics*, I/1, 403.
8 *Ibid.*, 137, citing Barth from *Church Dogmatics*, I/1, 438 f.
9 *Ibid.*, 137.
10 *Ibid.*, 139.
11 *Ibid.*, 140.
12 *Ibid.*, 141, again citing Barth from *Church Dogmatics*, I/1, 158.
13 *Ibid.*, 141.
14 *Ibid.*, 141.
15 Brian Leftow, "Anti Social Trinitarianism" in *The Trinity: An Interdisciplinary Study of the Doctrine of the Trinity* (ed. Stephen T. Davis, Daniel Kendall and Gerald O'Collins; Oxford: OUP, 1999), 203–49.
16 Baillie, *God was in Christ*, 142, cf. Lewis Ayres making a similar point about the Cappadocian commitment to unity: 'Gregory of Nyssa's small text *On Not Three Gods* has often been treated as a key statement of his supposedly "pluralistic" and/or "social" Trinitarianism. I argue, first, that Gregory's intention here is to shift discussion away from a focus on the possible analogies between the

divine life and three seemingly distinct human beings, toward themes more fundamental in his theology. Second, I offer a reading of *On Not Three Gods* to show how Gregory's Trinitarian theology—as all pro-Nicene theologies— revolves around a strong commitment to the unity of the divine power and activity and an equally strong insistence that all statements about the divine life and persons are governed by an account of the divine incomprehensibility'. Lewis Ayres, "On Not Three People: The Fundamental Themes of Gregory of Nyssa's Trinitarian Theology as Seen in *To Ablabius: On Not Three Gods*," *Modern Theology* 18 (2002): 445–74.

17 Baillie, *God was in Christ*, 142, again essentially in agreement with Ayres.

18 See their respective articles in *Modern Theology* 18 (2002). See also the article by Sarah Coakley, "'Persons' in the 'Social' Doctrine of the Trinity: A Critique of Current Analytic Discussion" in Davis, Kendall and O'Collins, *The Trinity*, but especially Lucian Turcescu, "'Person' versus "Individual", and Other Modern Misreadings of Gregory of Nyssa' in the same *Modern Theology* volume (pp. 527–39) where he argues that 'despite claiming that his own ontology of personhood is patristic-based, Zizioulas has not convincingly exegeted the Cappadocian theology of person, especially that of Gregory of Nyssa and Basil of Caesarea. This is unfortunate, given the fact that there are dozens of patristic quotations from, or references to, various Greek Fathers (especially the Cappadocians) throughout Zizioulas's works. Instead, he uses nineteenth- and twentieth-century insights which he then foists on the Cappadocians. This methodology leads him to misleading conclusions. ... Zizioulas is therefore in error when he contends that the Cappadocians did not understand a person as an individual or when he credits them with having had the same concerns we moderns have when combating individualism today.' (p. 536 f.).

19 Baillie, *God was in Christ*, 147.

20 J. P. Mackey, *The Christian Experience of God as Trinity* (London: SCM Press, 1983), 192.

21 For example see Jürgen Moltmann's discussion of Barth and Rahner in these terms in *The Trinity and the Kingdom of God*, 139–48.

22 Leonard Hodgson, *The Doctrine of the Trinity* (Welwyn: James Nisbet and Company, 1943), 157.

23 Augustine cited by Hodgson, *ibid.*, 154.

24 *Ibid.*, 155.

25 *Ibid.*

26 *Ibid.*, 156.

27 *Ibid.*, 164.

28 *Ibid.*

29 Sarah Coakley, "'Persons' in the 'Social' Doctrine of the Trinity," 131 f.

30 Sarah Coakley, "Re-thinking Gregory of Nyssa: Introduction—Gender,

Peter McEnhill

Trinitarian Analogies, and the Pedagogy of *The Song*," *Modern Theology* 18 (2002): 434.

31 *Ibid.*

32 John McIntyre, "The Holy Spirit in Greek Patristic Thought," *Scottish Journal of Theology* 7 (1954): 353 f., see also his more recent pronouncement in *The Shape of Pneumatology* (Edinburgh: T. & T. Clark, 1997), 87, where he writes "but it is central and primary to the Church's faith that the nature of God as Triad falls within the unity of God, the Triad being 'one and indivisible'. So I cannot agree with S. L. Prestige (*God in Patristic Thought*, SPCK, London, 1964, p. 243) when he alleges that the Cappadocians accepted 'objective triplicity' as the basis of their thought, and that 'identity of divine *ousia*' was for them second in importance."

33 Mackey, *The Christian Experience of God as Trinity*, 144 f.

34 Moltmann, *The Trinity and the Kingdom of God.*

35 *Ibid.*, 144 and 148.

36 *Ibid.*, 57.

37 I say this notwithstanding Moltmann's rather cursory treatment of this subject in *The Trinity and the Kingdom of God*, 171 ff.

38 *Ibid.*, 60.

39 *Ibid.*, 175–6.

40 See Leftow's critique of David Brown and Richard Swinburne's treatments of 'social Trinitarianism' via what he terms 'group mind' and 'functional accounts of monotheism' in "Anti Social Trinitarianism," 221–31. Leftow's criticisms of 'social Trinitarianism' refine and strengthen Baillie's intuitive and much less highly refined and analytically developed critique of 'social Trinitarianism' in *God Was in Christ* – though Leftow, of course, is not consciously drawing upon Baillie as a resource.

41 Michel René Barnes, "Divine Unity and the Divided Self: Gregory of Nyssa's Trinitarian Theology in its Psychological Context," *Modern Theology* 18 (2002): 487.

42 *Ibid.*, 490.

43 John A. T. Robinson, "Thou who art" (PhD thesis, Cambridge University Library, 1946).

Contributors

WALTER BRUEGGEMANN, Professor emeritus of Old Testament at Columbia Theological Seminary, Decatur, Georgia, U.S.A.

EBERHARD BUSCH, Professor emeritus for Systematic Theology at the Georg-August-Universität, Göttingen, Germany.

MARTIN H. CRESSEY, formerly Principal of Westminster College, Cambridge.

DUNCAN B. FORRESTER, Professor emeritus of Practical Theology at the University of Edinburgh.

BRIAN A. GERRISH, formerly John Nuveen Professor in the Divinity School of the University of Chicago and Distinguished Service Professor of Theology, Union Theological Seminary & Presbyterian School of Christian Education, Richmond, Virginia, U.S.A.

COLIN GUNTON, late Professor of Christian Doctrine at King's College, the University of London.

PETER McENHILL, formerly Director of Studies in Systematic Theology at Westminster College, Cambridge.

JÜRGEN MOLTMANN, Professor emeritus of Systematic Theology at the University of Tübingen, Germany.

ALAN P. F. SELL, formerly Professor of Christian Doctrine and Philosophy of Religion at the United Theological College, Aberystwyth.